THROUGH TRIALS TO TRUTH

LESSONS ON SELF-AWARENESS

Made with ♥ on the Notion Press Platform
www.notionpress.com

To all the seekers of truth,
who bravely venture inward to understand themselves and the world around them.

This book is for those who face life's trials with resilience, embracing every challenge as an opportunity for growth.

To my family and friends, for their unwavering support and belief in me, and to every reader on this journey toward greater self-awareness — may these hard-earned truths serve as a guiding light on your path to deeper understanding and personal transformation.

With gratitude,
Dr. Anurag Tiwari

Contents

Foreword

Self-awareness is often considered the cornerstone of personal growth and emotional well-being. It's the ability to see oneself with clarity, recognizing both strengths and weaknesses, and it requires a lifelong commitment to introspection. But self-awareness is not easily achieved; it's earned through experiences, struggles, and the willingness to confront our deepest truths.

In this book, "Hard-Earned Truths: Lessons on Self-Awareness," the journey toward understanding the self is explored with honesty and depth. The lessons presented are drawn from real-life challenges, moments of reflection, and transformative realizations. Each chapter invites the reader to not only examine their internal world but also to apply these insights to their everyday life—strengthening their relationships, decisions, and overall sense of purpose.

This work doesn't offer quick fixes or easy solutions. Instead, it guides you through the process of understanding who you are at your core, navigating your emotions, and aligning your actions with your true self. As you read, you'll discover that self-awareness isn't about perfection but about embracing your imperfections and growing through them.

I believe this book will serve as a valuable companion for anyone seeking a deeper connection with themselves. May the hard-earned truths within these pages inspire you to live authentically and with greater awareness of the unique path you are on.

With warmth and appreciation,
Dr.Anurag Tiwari

Preface

The path to self-awareness is a deeply personal and often challenging one. It demands honesty, vulnerability, and the courage to face both the brightest and darkest parts of who we are. As I began my own journey of self-discovery, I quickly realized that the most profound lessons weren't found in books or lectures but through lived experiences—the triumphs, the failures, the heartbreaks, and the moments of quiet reflection.

"Hard-Earned Truths: Lessons on Self-Awareness" is born from these experiences. It is a collection of insights gathered over time, often through trials and errors, as I learned to navigate life's complexities. These lessons are not theoretical but practical and real, shaped by personal growth, reflection, and the constant push to better understand myself and my place in the world.

In writing this book, my hope is to share these hard-earned truths with others who may be on similar journeys. The lessons here are not exhaustive, nor do they claim to offer a universal solution. Rather, they are intended as a guide—one that encourages you to ask deeper questions, to pause, and to reflect on the many layers of your own life.

This book is for anyone willing to explore the terrain of their inner world, to confront their insecurities, and to celebrate their strengths. It is for those who believe that self-awareness is not a destination but a continual process of growth and understanding. I hope that as you turn these pages, you will find something that resonates with your own experiences and supports you on your journey toward a more authentic and fulfilled life.

Thank you for joining me on this exploration of self-awareness. May these hard-earned truths inspire you to embrace all that you are—and all that you can become.

With appreciation,
Dr.Anurag Tiwari

Acknowledgements

This book wouldn't have been possible without the support, guidance, and inspiration of so many remarkable people. First and foremost, I want to thank my family, whose love and encouragement have been the foundation of everything I do. Your unwavering belief in me kept me going, especially during the times when self-doubt crept in.

To my friends and mentors, thank you for your wisdom, honesty, and perspective. Your willingness to share your own hard-earned truths helped shape the lessons in these pages. You've inspired me not only to learn from my experiences but also to see the value in every setback and success.

To my readers—whether you're just starting your journey toward self-awareness or have been at it for years—thank you for picking up this book. Writing for you has been a deeply personal and rewarding experience. I hope the insights shared here resonate with you and provide clarity in your own path of self-discovery.

A special thank you to my editor and publishing team, whose skill and dedication helped bring this book to life. Your feedback, patience, and expertise have been invaluable throughout this process.

Lastly, to life itself—the ups, the downs, and everything in between—thank you for teaching me the most profound lessons, even when I wasn't ready to learn them. Every experience, no matter how challenging, has been part of this journey, and I am grateful for the growth it has brought.

With deepest gratitude,

Dr.Anurag Tiwari

Prologue

We all have moments when life forces us to look inward—whether through a failure, a loss, or a quiet realization that something isn't right. These moments are often uncomfortable, but they are also where real growth happens. In the quiet of those reflective moments, we encounter the truths about ourselves that we often try to avoid or overlook.

Self-awareness is not a destination but a process—a gradual peeling back of the layers that we've accumulated over time. It's in those moments of honesty with ourselves that we can see things clearly: our motivations, our fears, our strengths, and our blind spots. But getting to that place isn't easy. It takes effort, vulnerability, and the courage to face parts of ourselves we might not want to confront.

This book is a testament to the idea that self-awareness is earned, not given. It's the result of countless hard-earned truths—moments when life throws challenges our way, and we're forced to learn, adapt, and grow. These lessons, gathered through personal experiences and reflections, are meant to serve as guideposts for anyone seeking to better understand themselves.

Each of us carries within us the potential for self-awareness, but it's up to us to choose whether to engage with it. The road to self-awareness is not linear; it's full of detours, setbacks, and breakthroughs. But with every step, we inch closer to a fuller understanding of who we are and how we navigate the world.

As you read these lessons, I hope they inspire you to look inward and embrace your own journey toward greater self-awareness. Remember, the path is yours, and the truths you uncover along the way are what make the journey worthwhile.

Welcome to the beginning of that journey.

Dr.Anurag Tiwari

ONE

The Journey of Life's Lessons:

Life is a continuous journey filled with moments of joy, hardship, growth, and transformation. Along this path, every experience—whether big or small—teaches us valuable lessons that shape who we are and guide us toward who we are becoming. The essence of life's lessons lies not just in the events themselves but in how we perceive, respond to, and grow from them. These lessons come in many forms—through relationships, personal challenges, moments of success, and even in silence and solitude. Some lessons are learned through reflection, while others are taught through adversity, urging us to dig deep into our resilience. The journey of life's lessons is not linear; it's cyclical, ever evolving, and unique to each individual. This book invites you to explore these lessons, reflect on your own path, and embrace the wisdom that life offers at every turn. Through this understanding, we not only grow but also find meaning and fulfillment in the world around us.

Understanding the Importance of Life's Teachings

Life, in all its complexity and unpredictability, is a masterful teacher. Each day offers us lessons—whether through triumphs, challenges, or seemingly mundane experiences. These lessons are not merely random occurrences; they are profound insights, messages, and guiding principles that shape our worldview, inform our decisions, and foster personal growth. Understanding the importance of life's teachings requires not only awareness but also an active willingness to learn from them, adapt, and grow. It is a conscious effort to derive meaning from experiences and use that meaning as fuel for self-improvement, empathy, and wisdom.

1. Life's Teachings as Catalysts for Personal Growth

Personal growth is one of the primary reasons why life's teachings hold such great importance. Growth, whether mental, emotional, or spiritual, is a continuous process. Life places us in situations that challenge our existing beliefs, habits, and perspectives, urging us to adapt and evolve. Each difficult circumstance we face, from small inconveniences to significant obstacles, becomes a powerful teaching moment. For example, facing failure teaches us resilience and perseverance. It demonstrates that success is often the result of persistence, learning from setbacks, and having the courage to try again.

One of the greatest gifts life gives us is the understanding that we are always capable of change. No matter how ingrained a particular behavior or mindset may be, life teaches us that change is possible when we are open to learning and evolving. Recognizing this encourages a growth mindset, where we see challenges not as barriers but as opportunities to learn and become better versions of ourselves. When we view life's lessons as stepping stones for personal growth, we gain the ability to transcend our limitations and become more self-aware, compassionate, and adaptive.

2. Life's Lessons Build Resilience and Adaptability

Life is full of uncertainties, and it often presents us with unexpected challenges. Whether it's the loss of a loved one, a career setback, or a personal disappointment, these events test our resilience. Resilience—the ability to bounce back from adversity—is not something we are born with but a quality we develop over time through life's teachings. Every time we overcome a hardship; we strengthen our ability to cope with future challenges.

Resilience is closely tied to adaptability. Life's lessons teach us to adapt to changing circumstances, which is essential in a world that is constantly evolving. For instance, in the face of technological advancements, economic shifts, or personal crises, our ability to adapt determines our success and happiness. Adaptability is about learning to let go of rigid expectations and being open to change. Life teaches us that the more flexible and adaptable we are, the better we can navigate difficult situations and find creative solutions to problems.

3. Learning from Failure: A Powerful Teacher

Failure is one of the most powerful teachers in life. While society often emphasizes success, it is failure that provides the most profound lessons. Failure humbles us, forcing us to confront our limitations and encouraging us to rethink our strategies. When we fail, we are given the opportunity to reflect on what went wrong, why it happened, and what can be done differently next time.

The importance of learning from failure lies in the fact that it fosters resilience, perseverance, and innovation. Many of the world's greatest achievements have been born out of failure. Famous inventors, entrepreneurs, and leaders have often cited their failures as pivotal moments in their journeys. Thomas Edison, for example, famously failed thousands of times before successfully inventing the light bulb. He viewed each failure not as a defeat but as a step closer to success, saying, "I have not failed. I've just found 10,000 ways that won't work."

Failure also teaches us the importance of humility and patience. It reminds us that success is not always immediate, and that persistence is key. When we understand the value of failure, we stop fearing it and start embracing it as a necessary part of the learning process.

4. Empathy and Compassion: Life's Lessons Through Relationships

Life teaches us valuable lessons about empathy and compassion through our relationships with others. Every interaction, whether with family, friends, colleagues, or strangers, presents an opportunity to understand different perspectives and cultivate empathy. Relationships often challenge us to put ourselves in others' shoes, to listen deeply, and to offer support in times of need.

Compassion is a lesson that life teaches us repeatedly, often through personal experiences of pain or hardship. When we go through difficult times, we become more compassionate toward others who may be experiencing similar struggles. This shared sense of humanity fosters deeper connections and allows us to offer kindness and support to those around us.

Furthermore, relationships teach us the importance of forgiveness and letting go of grudges. Holding onto anger or resentment only hinders our growth and happiness. Life's lessons encourage us to forgive, not because the other person necessarily deserves it, but because it frees us from the emotional burden of negativity. In doing so, we learn to cultivate inner peace and move forward with greater emotional freedom.

5. Life Teaches Us to Embrace Uncertainty

One of the most difficult yet essential lessons that life teaches us is to embrace uncertainty. We often seek control over our lives, wanting to plan every detail and predict every outcome. However, life is inherently unpredictable. Events rarely unfold exactly as we expect, and this unpredictability can lead to feelings of anxiety or fear. Yet, it is precisely in these moments of uncertainty that life teaches us to trust the process.

Embracing uncertainty involves letting go of the need for control and learning to be present in the moment. It teaches us to adapt to whatever comes our way with grace and resilience. When we stop resisting the unknown and instead accept it as a natural part of life, we experience greater peace and freedom. The lesson here is that while we cannot control everything that happens, we can control how we respond to it. This mindset allows us to navigate uncertainty with confidence and courage.

6. Gratitude: The Power of Appreciation

Gratitude is one of the most transformative lessons life teaches us. When we practice gratitude, we shift our focus from what we lack to what we have. This shift in perspective has a profound impact on our overall happiness and well-being. Life's lessons often come in the form of small, everyday moments that we might otherwise overlook. The beauty of a sunset, the warmth of a smile, the comfort of a home—these are all gifts that life offers us.

By cultivating a habit of gratitude, we learn to appreciate life's simple pleasures and recognize the abundance that surrounds us. Gratitude also helps us to reframe challenges and hardships. Even in difficult times, there is always something to be thankful for. This practice of gratitude allows us to find meaning and positivity, even in the face of adversity.

7. Purpose and Fulfillment: Lessons in Meaning

Life teaches us that true fulfillment comes from living a life of purpose. Purpose is not something that is handed to us; it is something we discover through our experiences, passions, and contributions to the world. Finding purpose often involves trial and error, as we explore different paths and learn what resonates with our values and desires.

Living with purpose gives our lives direction and meaning. It motivates us to pursue goals that align with our values and to contribute to something greater than ourselves. Whether it's through our careers, relationships, or acts of service, living with purpose brings a deep sense of satisfaction and fulfillment. Life's lessons often point us toward our purpose by showing us what truly matters and what brings us joy.

8. Mindfulness: Being Present in the Moment

One of the most profound lessons life teaches is the importance of mindfulness—being present in the moment. In a fast-paced world where we are constantly distracted by technology, work, and responsibilities, mindfulness encourages us to slow down and fully experience the present. Life's teachings often come in subtle, fleeting moments, and it is only by being present that we can truly appreciate them.

Mindfulness helps us to cultivate a deeper awareness of our thoughts, feelings, and surroundings. It allows us to connect more meaningfully with ourselves and others. Through mindfulness, we learn to savor life's simple pleasures and find peace amidst the chaos.

9. Embracing Life's Teachings

Understanding the importance of life's teachings is not about seeking perfection but about recognizing the value of every experience, both positive and negative. Life is constantly teaching us lessons that guide us toward personal growth, resilience, empathy, and fulfillment. By embracing these lessons with an open heart and mind, we allow ourselves to evolve into the best versions of ourselves.

Ultimately, life's teachings are about fostering a deeper connection with ourselves, others, and the world around us. They remind us that every moment is an opportunity to learn, grow, and live with greater purpose, gratitude, and mindfulness. As we journey through life, these teachings become the compass that guides us toward a more meaningful and fulfilling existence.

How We Learn from Experience

Experience is one of life's most powerful teachers. It shapes our understanding, informs our decisions, and molds our character in ways that no book or lecture can fully replicate. Learning from experience is a process that allows us to derive wisdom and insights from our own lives, drawing lessons from both successes and failures. Unlike passive learning, where we simply absorb information, experiential learning requires active engagement. It is through lived experience that we internalize knowledge, develop skills, and gain the capacity to handle life's complexities with greater awareness and resilience.

This essay explores how we learn from experience, the different types of experiences that shape our understanding, and the methods by which we can maximize the lessons they offer. By delving into the intricate relationship between experience, reflection, and personal growth, we come to appreciate the profound role experience plays in guiding us toward a more enriched and enlightened life.

1. The Role of Experience in Learning

Experience is a bridge between theoretical knowledge and practical application. While formal education provides us with frameworks and ideas, it is experience that tests these ideas in real-life scenarios. This process of applying knowledge to the real world often leads to unexpected challenges, nuances, and insights that deepen our understanding. For example, learning about business strategies in a classroom setting offers valuable concepts, but it is only through actually running a business—managing people, handling finances, and responding to market changes—that one truly grasps the complexities of entrepreneurship.

This process of learning through doing is sometimes referred to as *experiential learning*. Psychologist David Kolb's Experiential Learning Theory (ELT) outlines this as a cyclical process involving four stages: concrete experience, reflective observation, abstract conceptualization, and active experimentation. In other words, we engage with an experience, reflect on what happened, analyze it to develop broader insights, and then use those insights to guide future actions. This cycle repeats with each new experience, continuously refining our understanding and abilities.

2. Learning Through Success and Achievement

One of the most gratifying ways to learn from experience is through success. Achievements reinforce the notion that our decisions, efforts, and strategies were effective, giving us a sense of competence and confidence. When we succeed, we validate the skills and approaches we employed, and this positive feedback motivates us to continue refining and applying those strategies.

However, success is more than just a reward; it is a learning tool. Each successful outcome offers an opportunity to analyze the factors that contributed to the positive result. For instance, an athlete who wins a race may reflect on the quality of their training, the strategies they employed during the competition, and their mental state before and during the event. By identifying the elements that led to success, they can replicate or even enhance these strategies in future competitions.

Success also teaches us about perseverance. Often, accomplishments are the culmination of sustained effort over time. By recognizing that success is not merely a stroke of luck but the result of dedication and hard work, we learn the importance of discipline, consistency, and resilience in achieving our goals.

3. Learning Through Failure and Mistakes

While success is a powerful teacher, failure is arguably an even more profound source of learning. When we fail, we are forced to confront our limitations, mistakes, and areas for improvement. Failure strips away illusions and highlights the gaps in our knowledge, skills, or strategies. It is often in these moments of vulnerability that we gain the most significant insights.

Failures compel us to engage in self-reflection, a critical component of experiential learning. Reflecting on failure involves asking key questions: What went wrong? What could I have done differently? What external factors influenced the outcome? These questions help us identify the root causes of failure, and from these answers, we can develop a more informed approach to similar situations in the future.

A common barrier to learning from failure is the tendency to avoid it. Many people fear failure because it is associated with pain, embarrassment, or the feeling of inadequacy. However, those who embrace failure as a learning opportunity develop resilience and a growth mindset—the belief that abilities can be developed through effort and learning. Thomas Edison, the inventor of the lightbulb, famously said, "I have not failed. I've just found 10,000 ways that won't work." His perspective illustrates how failure can be reframed as a necessary step toward success.

Failure also teaches us the value of humility and patience. While success may boost our confidence, failure reminds us that we still have much to learn. It teaches us that growth is often a slow, iterative process and that we must be patient with ourselves as we continue to develop our abilities and understanding.

4. The Importance of Reflection in Experiential Learning

Experience alone does not automatically result in learning. For experience to be meaningful, it must be accompanied by reflection. Reflection is the process of looking back on an experience, analyzing it, and drawing lessons from it. Without reflection, we risk repeating the same mistakes or failing to recognize the factors that contributed to our successes.

Reflective practice is essential for both personal and professional development. In the workplace, for example, employees and leaders alike are encouraged to engage in post-project reviews or performance evaluations. These structured reflections allow teams to analyze what worked, what didn't, and how future projects can be improved. In personal life, journaling or discussing experiences with trusted friends or mentors can serve as a form of reflection, helping individuals process their emotions and derive insights from their experiences.

Reflection also fosters self-awareness, a key component of emotional intelligence. By reflecting on how we responded to certain situations, we become more attuned to our emotional triggers, strengths, and weaknesses. This self-awareness enables us to manage our emotions more effectively and make better decisions in the future.

5. Learning Through Observation and Social Interaction

While personal experience is invaluable, we also learn from the experiences of others. Observing how others navigate challenges, solve problems, and achieve success provides us with models for our own behavior. This form of learning, known as *observational learning*, allows us to benefit from the wisdom of others without having to experience every situation firsthand.

Social interactions play a critical role in this process. Through conversations, collaborations, and shared experiences, we gain new perspectives and insights that enhance our understanding of the world. Mentorship, for example, is a powerful way to learn from someone else's experiences. A mentor can provide guidance, share their own successes and failures, and offer advice based on their life's lessons.

In addition to direct observation, we can learn vicariously through literature, history, and art. Stories of historical figures, for example, provide us with examples of leadership, courage, and innovation. By studying their lives, we learn valuable lessons about decision-making, resilience, and the impact of one's actions on society. Literature, too, offers insights into the human condition, allowing us to explore the complexities of relationships, morality, and personal growth through the experiences of fictional characters.

6. The Role of Emotions in Experiential Learning

Emotions play a significant role in how we learn from experience. Experiences that evoke strong emotions—whether joy, fear, sadness, or anger—tend to leave a lasting impact on our memory and understanding. For example, the exhilaration of achieving a long-term goal reinforces the value of persistence, while the pain of a personal loss teaches us about the fragility of life and the importance of cherishing relationships.

Emotionally charged experiences also provide opportunities for developing emotional intelligence. Emotional intelligence involves recognizing, understanding, and managing our emotions as well as the emotions of others. Through emotional experiences, we learn to navigate complex social situations, develop empathy, and improve our communication skills.

Moreover, emotions act as internal feedback mechanisms. Positive emotions signal that we are on the right path, while negative emotions indicate that something is amiss. By paying attention to our emotional responses, we can better understand our needs, desires, and values, and make decisions that align with our well-being.

7. The Role of Time in Learning from Experience

Learning from experience is not always immediate. Sometimes, the lessons embedded in an experience only become clear with the passage of time. In the midst of a challenging situation, we may be too overwhelmed by emotions or circumstances to fully comprehend the lesson at hand. However, as time passes, we gain distance and perspective, allowing us to reflect more objectively on what occurred and why.

This is why patience is an essential component of experiential learning. We must allow ourselves the time and space to process our experiences fully, without rushing to conclusions. Sometimes, the most valuable lessons are those that emerge slowly, through deep reflection and contemplation.

Furthermore, repeated exposure to certain experiences over time allows us to refine our understanding and improve our responses. For example, a teacher's first year in the classroom may be fraught with challenges, but with each subsequent year, they become more adept at managing students, creating effective lesson plans, and fostering a positive learning environment. Over time, experience sharpens our instincts and hones our skills.

8. Applying Lessons from Experience to Future Actions

The ultimate goal of learning from experience is to apply the lessons we've learned to future actions. Experience teaches us not only what to do but also what to avoid. By reflecting on past experiences, we can make more informed decisions, anticipate potential challenges, and create better outcomes.

This process of applying lessons from experience involves continuous experimentation and adaptation. Each new situation presents a unique set of variables, and while past experiences provide valuable guidance, they cannot dictate our actions entirely. Instead, we must remain open to new possibilities and be willing to adjust our approach as needed.

For example, a manager who has successfully led a team in one organization may find that the same leadership style does not work in a different company culture. While their past experiences provide a foundation for their leadership skills, they must remain flexible and responsive to the specific needs of their new team. This adaptability is a hallmark of experiential learning and is key to long-term success.

Embracing Growth through Reflection

Growth is an inherent part of life, and it's something we all strive for, whether consciously or unconsciously. However, growth doesn't happen by chance. It requires awareness, effort, and, most importantly, reflection. Reflection is the practice of thoughtfully considering our experiences, actions, and responses, enabling us to draw lessons from them. By reflecting on our lives, we engage in a process that deepens our self-awareness, enhances our emotional intelligence, and sharpens our decision-making abilities. Embracing growth through reflection empowers us to transform our experiences into meaningful learning opportunities, driving personal and professional development.

This essay will explore the concept of reflection as a powerful tool for growth, the methods of reflective practice, and the profound effects it can have on both personal and collective well-being. Through the lens of self-reflection, we can uncover the power of mindfulness, emotional understanding, and continuous improvement, all of which contribute to a more fulfilling life.

1. The Role of Reflection in Personal Growth

Reflection is more than just thinking about our past. It is a deliberate and structured process that involves analyzing our actions, emotions, and thoughts to gain deeper insights. This process of introspection allows us to understand the "why" behind our decisions and behaviors, leading to heightened self-awareness and, ultimately, personal growth.

Personal growth begins with awareness. Without an understanding of who we are—our strengths, weaknesses, habits, and tendencies—we cannot initiate meaningful change. Reflection offers a mirror through which we can observe ourselves more objectively. By stepping back and examining our thoughts and actions, we can begin to identify patterns that may be holding us back or propelling us forward.

For instance, consider someone who continually faces conflicts in their relationships. Through reflection, they might realize that their communication style—perhaps one that is overly critical or defensive—is contributing to these problems. With this newfound awareness, they can work on adopting a more compassionate and constructive approach to communication. The act of reflecting on past behaviors serves as a catalyst for growth, allowing individuals to change their habits and behaviors for the better.

2. Reflection and Emotional Intelligence

Emotional intelligence (EI) refers to the ability to recognize, understand, and manage our own emotions, as well as to empathize with and influence the emotions of others. It is a key component of successful relationships and effective leadership. Reflection plays a crucial role in developing emotional intelligence because it allows us to analyze our emotional responses to different situations.

When we reflect on emotional experiences, we gain insight into how our emotions influence our behavior. For example, a manager may reflect on a tense meeting where they became frustrated with their team's lack of progress. Upon reflection, the manager might realize that their frustration stemmed from unrealistic expectations or personal stress unrelated to work. With this awareness, they can better manage their emotional reactions in future interactions and cultivate a more supportive and productive work environment.

Similarly, reflection helps us develop empathy by encouraging us to consider the emotions of others. By reflecting on how our words or actions might have affected someone else, we become more attuned to the feelings of others, leading to more compassionate and thoughtful interactions. As we grow in emotional intelligence through reflection, we enhance our relationships and create a more harmonious social environment.

3. The Practice of Mindful Reflection

Mindful reflection is a practice that combines the principles of mindfulness with reflective thinking. Mindfulness is the act of being fully present and engaged in the current moment, without judgment or distraction. When we apply mindfulness to reflection, we observe our thoughts and feelings with curiosity and openness, rather than criticism or defensiveness.

This practice of mindful reflection allows us to approach our experiences with greater clarity and objectivity. Instead of being swept away by emotions or biases, we can observe them calmly, gaining a clearer understanding of our inner world. For example, after a difficult day, we might take a few moments to sit quietly, close our eyes, and reflect on the emotions that surfaced throughout the day. By acknowledging these emotions without judgment, we can gain insight into what triggered them and how we can manage similar situations in the future.

Mindful reflection also helps us stay grounded in the present moment. Rather than getting stuck in regret over past mistakes or anxiety about the future, we focus on what we can learn from the present experience. This focus on the "here and now" encourages us to take actionable steps toward growth, rather than being paralyzed by rumination or fear.

4. Reflective Practice in Professional Development

In addition to fostering personal growth, reflection is also a critical component of professional development. Reflective practice, which involves analyzing work-related experiences to improve future performance, is widely used in fields such as education, healthcare, and leadership. By engaging in reflective practice, professionals are able to continuously refine their skills, adapt to changing environments, and provide higher-quality services.

One example of reflective practice in the workplace is the use of debriefs after significant events. In healthcare, for instance, medical teams often engage in post-operation reflections, where they discuss what went well during a procedure, what challenges were encountered, and how they can improve for future cases. These debriefs not only foster continuous learning but also enhance team communication and collaboration.

Leaders, too, benefit from reflective practice. By regularly reflecting on their leadership style, decision-making processes, and team dynamics, leaders can identify areas for improvement and make more informed decisions. Reflection allows them to be more aware of their impact on their teams, helping them foster a positive and productive work environment.

Moreover, reflective practice encourages innovation. When professionals reflect on challenges or failures, they are more likely to think critically about new solutions and approaches. This spirit of continuous improvement drives innovation and helps organizations stay competitive in a rapidly changing world.

5. Learning from Mistakes: The Power of Reflective Growth

One of the most significant benefits of reflection is its ability to transform mistakes into valuable learning opportunities. Everyone makes mistakes, but not everyone learns from them. It is through reflection that we gain the insights necessary to turn failures into growth experiences.

When we reflect on our mistakes, we move beyond feelings of shame or frustration and focus on the lessons they offer. For example, a business owner who experiences a failed product launch might initially feel disappointed or disheartened. However, by reflecting on the situation—analyzing the market research, marketing strategies, and customer feedback—they can identify what went wrong and how to avoid similar pitfalls in the future. This process of learning from mistakes enables them to grow stronger, wiser, and more prepared for future challenges.

Mistakes also teach us resilience. By reflecting on how we overcame past failures, we build confidence in our ability to handle adversity. This resilience is essential for personal and professional growth, as it allows us to face challenges with greater determination and a positive outlook.

6. Reflection as a Tool for Goal Setting and Achievement

Reflection is not only about looking back; it's also a powerful tool for looking forward. By reflecting on our past experiences, we gain clarity about our goals and aspirations. Reflection helps us assess what we truly want in life, what motivates us, and what steps we need to take to achieve our ambitions.

For instance, a student nearing graduation might reflect on their academic journey, considering the subjects they enjoyed most, the skills they developed, and the challenges they overcame. Through this reflective process, they can identify their strengths and passions, which in turn can guide their career choices and future goals.

Moreover, reflection allows us to evaluate our progress toward our goals. By regularly checking in with ourselves and reflecting on our actions, we can determine whether we are on the right path or whether adjustments are needed. This process of reflection ensures that our goals remain aligned with our values and that we are continuously moving in a direction that fosters personal and professional growth.

7. Cultivating a Habit of Reflection

While reflection is a powerful tool for growth, it requires conscious effort and practice to make it a regular part of our lives. Cultivating a habit of reflection involves setting aside time for introspection, being honest with ourselves, and approaching our experiences with an open mind.

One effective way to cultivate a habit of reflection is through journaling. Writing down our thoughts, feelings, and experiences encourages deeper self-exploration and allows us to track our progress over time. Journaling can also serve as a safe space for processing emotions and exploring new ideas, helping us make sense of complex or challenging situations.

Another method for cultivating reflection is engaging in regular conversations with trusted friends, mentors, or colleagues. These discussions can provide new perspectives and insights that we may not have considered on our own. By sharing our experiences and reflecting on them with others, we can gain a more comprehensive understanding of our actions and behaviors.

Mindfulness practices, such as meditation or deep breathing exercises, can also enhance our ability to reflect. These practices help us become more present and aware, allowing us to approach our reflections with greater clarity and focus.

8. The Collective Benefits of Reflective Growth

While reflection primarily fosters individual growth, it also has broader implications for collective well-being. When individuals engage in reflection and embrace personal growth, they contribute to healthier relationships, more productive workplaces, and stronger communities.

In relationships, reflection allows individuals to be more empathetic, understanding, and communicative. By reflecting on their own behaviors and emotions, they can identify ways to improve their interactions with others, leading to stronger and more fulfilling relationships. This, in turn, fosters a sense of connection and trust, which is essential for both personal and collective well-being.

In the workplace, reflective growth leads to more effective teamwork, leadership, and problem-solving. When employees and leaders alike engage in reflective practice, they create a culture of continuous learning and improvement. This culture not only enhances individual performance but also drives organizational success.

At a societal level, reflection encourages critical thinking and civic engagement. When individuals reflect on societal issues, they are more likely to challenge the status quo, advocate for change, and contribute to the greater good.

Embracing growth through reflection is a transformative process that empowers us to learn from our experiences, enhance our emotional intelligence, and achieve our personal and professional goals. By regularly engaging in reflective practices, we cultivate self-awareness, resilience, and empathy, all of which contribute to a more fulfilling and meaningful life. Moreover, the benefits of reflective growth extend beyond the individual, fostering healthier relationships, more productive workplaces, and stronger communities. As we continue to reflect, learn, and grow, we unlock our full potential and create a positive impact on the world around us.

TWO

Part I: Lessons on Self-Awareness

Self-awareness is the cornerstone of personal growth, the foundation upon which all other life lessons are built. To know oneself is to engage in a deep and honest exploration of one's thoughts, emotions, strengths, and weaknesses. This journey requires stepping back from the noise of daily life and critically reflecting on who we are at our core. By embracing self-awareness, we gain the clarity to understand our motivations, recognize our triggers, and see how our actions impact ourselves and others. It empowers us to make intentional choices that align with our values and aspirations. In "Know Thyself," the first step in this journey, we learn that true self-awareness isn't a destination but a lifelong practice, one that continuously reveals new layers of insight and growth. Through reflection, we unlock the power to shape our lives with purpose, authenticity, and integrity.

The Power of Self-Reflection

Self-reflection is one of the most powerful tools available for personal development and growth. It involves the conscious act of looking inward—examining one's thoughts, behaviors, emotions, and motivations. By engaging in self-reflection, individuals are able to gain deeper insights into themselves, understand the reasons behind their actions, and make more informed decisions. This process fosters self-awareness, emotional intelligence, and continuous self-improvement, all of which are essential for achieving long-term success and fulfillment in both personal and professional aspects of life.

Self-reflection is not just a passive review of events but an active process of questioning and learning. It involves asking difficult questions, confronting uncomfortable truths, and recognizing patterns that may be holding us back. When we commit to regularly engaging in self-reflection, we open ourselves to new possibilities, growth, and understanding, transforming our lives from within. This essay will explore the importance of self-reflection, its benefits, how to cultivate it, and how it leads to greater self-awareness, resilience, and personal growth.

1. The Importance of Self-Reflection

At its core, self-reflection is a process of introspection, where individuals analyze their experiences to gain clarity and insight. The modern world is fast-paced, and many people move from one task to the next without taking the time to pause and evaluate their actions. This lack of reflection can lead to feelings of disconnection, dissatisfaction, or being "stuck" in certain patterns. By making time for self-reflection, we give ourselves the opportunity to learn from our experiences and apply those lessons to future situations.

One of the key reasons self-reflection is so important is that it allows us to better understand our emotional responses and behavior patterns. Often, we react to situations based on past experiences or ingrained habits without fully recognizing the triggers that influence our behavior. Through self-reflection, we can dissect our emotional responses, uncover the root causes of those reactions, and adjust our behavior accordingly. This process promotes emotional intelligence, allowing us to better manage our emotions and improve our interactions with others.

Additionally, self-reflection enhances decision-making. In both personal and professional realms, the decisions we make have a profound impact on our lives. By reflecting on past decisions, successes, and failures, we can improve our ability to make sound judgments in the future. Reflection helps us recognize the factors that influenced our past decisions and allows us to approach similar situations with greater wisdom and clarity.

2. The Benefits of Self-Reflection

The benefits of self-reflection extend far beyond improved decision-making. This practice leads to a deeper understanding of oneself and cultivates emotional resilience, self-awareness, and personal growth.

a. **Self-Awareness :** Self-awareness is one of the most significant benefits of self-reflection. By engaging in regular reflection, individuals can better understand their values, goals, strengths, and weaknesses. This level of self-awareness is critical for personal and professional success because it allows individuals to align their actions with their true selves. When we are aware of who we are and what we want, we are better equipped to make choices that serve our best interests and lead to a more authentic and fulfilling life.

Self-awareness also allows individuals to identify patterns of behavior that may be holding them back. For example, through reflection, one might notice a tendency to procrastinate or avoid difficult conversations. By recognizing these patterns, individuals can take proactive steps to change them and develop more productive habits.

a. **Emotional Resilience**

Self-reflection builds emotional resilience by helping individuals process and understand their emotions. In the face of adversity, many people experience intense emotions such as frustration, anger, or sadness. Without reflection, these emotions can linger and lead to negative behaviors. However, when individuals take the time to reflect on their emotional responses, they can gain a clearer understanding of what triggered those emotions and how to manage them effectively.

For instance, after a stressful day at work, reflecting on the source of the stress can reveal whether it was caused by external factors, such as an overwhelming workload, or internal factors, such as perfectionism or self-doubt. By recognizing the source of the emotion, individuals can develop strategies to cope with stress in healthier and more productive ways. This process of emotional reflection builds resilience, allowing individuals to bounce back more quickly from challenges and setbacks.

c. **Personal Growth and Development** :One of the most significant benefits of self-reflection is its ability to foster personal growth and development. Growth is a continuous process that requires learning from experiences and applying those lessons to future situations. Through self-reflection, individuals can identify areas for improvement, set new goals, and take actionable steps toward achieving them.

For example, someone who aspires to improve their communication skills might reflect on recent conversations to evaluate how effectively they conveyed their thoughts and emotions. By identifying areas where they could have communicated more clearly or listened more attentively, they can work on developing those skills in future interactions.

Self-reflection also encourages a growth mindset, which is the belief that abilities and intelligence can be developed through effort and learning.

By reflecting on mistakes and challenges, individuals can view them as opportunities for growth rather than as failures. This shift in perspective promotes a more positive and proactive approach to personal development.

3. Cultivating the Habit of Self-Reflection

While self-reflection is a powerful tool, it requires conscious effort and practice to make it a habit. Cultivating the habit of self-reflection involves setting aside dedicated time for introspection, being open to self-examination, and creating a structured approach to reflection.

a. **Setting Time for Reflection** :In today's busy world, finding time for self-reflection can be challenging. However, it is essential to prioritize reflection as part of a daily or weekly routine. Setting aside even just 10-15 minutes each day for reflection can have a significant impact on personal growth. Whether it's in the morning before starting the day or in the evening before bed, creating a consistent time for reflection helps ensure that it becomes a regular practice.

During this time, it's important to eliminate distractions and create a quiet space for introspection. This allows for a focused and meaningful reflection process, where individuals can delve into their thoughts and emotions without interruptions.

b. **Journaling** : One of the most effective methods for self-reflection is journaling. Writing down thoughts, feelings, and experiences helps individuals organize their reflections and provides a tangible record of their progress over time. Journaling encourages deeper exploration of emotions and events, allowing individuals to uncover patterns and insights that might not be immediately apparent through casual reflection.

When journaling, it's helpful to ask specific questions to guide the reflection process. Questions such as, "What went well today?" "What could I have done differently?" "How did I feel in that situation?" and "What did I learn?" encourage thoughtful analysis and self-exploration. Regularly reviewing past journal entries also provides valuable insights into personal growth and development.

c. **Mindfulness and Meditation:** Mindfulness and meditation are powerful tools for enhancing self-reflection. These practices encourage individuals to become more present and aware of their thoughts and emotions in the moment. By cultivating mindfulness, individuals can approach reflection with greater clarity and focus, making it easier to understand their inner world.

Meditation, in particular, promotes a sense of calm and stillness that is conducive to deep reflection. Even just a few minutes of meditation each day can help individuals clear their minds and create space for meaningful introspection.

d. Seeking Feedback from Others: While self-reflection is primarily an internal process, seeking feedback from trusted friends, mentors, or colleagues can provide valuable insights that might not be apparent from self-reflection alone. Other people's perspectives can offer new angles of understanding and challenge any blind spots or biases we may have.

Engaging in reflective conversations with others allows individuals to gain different perspectives on their experiences and behaviors. These discussions can lead to greater self-awareness and more well-rounded personal growth.

4. The Transformative Power of Self-Reflection

Self-reflection has the potential to transform lives by fostering self-awareness, emotional intelligence, and personal growth. The more individuals engage in self-reflection, the more they are able to understand themselves and navigate life's challenges with greater wisdom and resilience.

One of the most transformative aspects of self-reflection is its ability to change how individuals perceive themselves and their experiences. Through reflection, individuals can reframe negative experiences or mistakes as opportunities for growth. This shift in perspective empowers individuals to approach challenges with a positive and proactive mindset, leading to greater success and fulfillment.

For example, a person who experiences failure in their career might initially feel discouraged and defeated. However, through self-reflection, they can analyze the factors that contributed to the failure and identify areas for improvement. This reflection process not only helps them learn from the experience but also builds resilience, allowing them to approach future challenges with renewed confidence and determination.

Self-reflection also fosters greater empathy and compassion, both for oneself and others. By reflecting on one's own emotions and experiences, individuals develop a deeper understanding of the human condition and become more empathetic toward others' struggles. This empathy enhances relationships, promotes kindness, and fosters a more supportive and connected community.

The power of self-reflection lies in its ability to unlock deeper self-awareness, foster emotional resilience, and promote continuous personal growth. By regularly engaging in reflective practices such as journaling, mindfulness, and seeking feedback, individuals can gain valuable insights into their thoughts, behaviors, and emotions. This process of introspection leads to greater clarity, improved decision-making, and more meaningful personal and professional development.

Ultimately, self-reflection is a transformative practice that empowers individuals to take control of their lives, make intentional choices, and grow into their best selves. As we embrace the power of self-reflection, we open the door to a life of purpose, fulfillment, and lasting growth.

Embracing Strengths and Weaknesses

Embracing our strengths and weaknesses is fundamental to personal growth, self-acceptance, and overall success. We often focus on either trying to maximize our strengths or hiding our weaknesses, but true self-empowerment comes from acknowledging both in equal measure. Understanding and accepting our strengths and weaknesses allows us to become more self-aware, balanced, and resilient, enabling us to navigate challenges and achieve our goals more effectively. This balance is not just about self-criticism or self-praise but about using our strengths wisely and working on our weaknesses for growth.

This essay will explore the importance of identifying and embracing our strengths and weaknesses, how we can use them to our advantage, and how they contribute to our personal and professional lives.

1. The Value of Recognizing Strengths

Our strengths are the qualities, skills, and talents that we excel in. They are often the aspects of our personality and abilities that come most naturally to us, and they represent areas where we can shine. Recognizing our strengths is vital because they form the foundation of our personal power and identity. When we embrace our strengths, we unlock the potential for success in various areas of life, from relationships to career and personal fulfillment.

One of the key benefits of identifying strengths is that it allows us to focus our energy where we can have the greatest impact. When we know what we're good at, we can lean into those abilities and contribute more effectively, both in personal endeavors and professional environments. For example, a person who excels at communication can leverage that strength to become a great leader, advocate, or negotiator.

Furthermore, using our strengths builds confidence. When we know we're good at something, we're more likely to take on challenges and pursue opportunities that align with those strengths. Confidence breeds more success, creating a positive cycle of achievement and self-esteem.

Another important aspect of recognizing strengths is the ability to use them to help others. Our strengths not only serve our personal goals but can also be a source of support and inspiration to those around us. For instance, a person with strong organizational skills can assist a team in becoming more efficient, while someone with excellent empathy can help resolve conflicts and build stronger relationships.

2. The Importance of Acknowledging Weaknesses

While it's important to celebrate and use our strengths, it is equally essential to acknowledge our weaknesses. Weaknesses are often viewed negatively, but they are a natural part of being human. Everyone has areas where they struggle or where they are not as skilled or competent. The key to personal growth is not to ignore these weaknesses but to recognize them as opportunities for improvement.

Acknowledging our weaknesses allows us to be more honest with ourselves and others. It fosters self-awareness and humility, two essential traits for continuous growth. When we admit that we are not perfect and that there are areas where we can improve, we open ourselves up to learning and development. This process helps us become more adaptable and resilient, as we're not held back by the fear of failure or inadequacy.

One of the greatest benefits of acknowledging weaknesses is that it allows us to seek help and support. When we know where we need improvement, we can seek guidance, mentorship, or training in those areas. For example, someone who struggles with time management might benefit from learning new organizational techniques or seeking advice from a colleague who excels in that area. By being open about our weaknesses, we create a collaborative environment where we can learn from others.

Moreover, recognizing weaknesses can prevent overextending ourselves. Many people feel the pressure to be good at everything, leading to burnout and frustration. However, when we accept that we can't excel in every area, we can focus our energy on what truly matters and delegate tasks where necessary. This mindset not only reduces stress but also allows us to function more efficiently.

3. Balancing Strengths and Weaknesses

Balancing strengths and weaknesses is an ongoing process that involves self-awareness, adaptability, and reflection. While we should certainly aim to maximize our strengths, we must also put effort into improving our weaknesses in ways that promote growth rather than overwhelm.

One effective way to balance strengths and weaknesses is through reflection and feedback. Regularly reflecting on our experiences helps us recognize patterns in our behaviors, strengths, and areas for improvement. Seeking feedback from trusted friends, colleagues, or mentors can provide us with valuable insights into areas we might not see clearly ourselves. This feedback helps us gain perspective and refine our approach to personal development.

Setting realistic goals is also essential in balancing strengths and weaknesses. Goals that challenge us without overburdening us can create a healthy balance between building on our strengths and addressing our weaknesses. For example, someone who is naturally good at public speaking but struggles with preparation might set a goal to become better at planning their presentations, thus combining a strength (public speaking) with a weakness (preparation).

Balancing strengths and weaknesses also requires embracing a growth mindset. A growth mindset is the belief that abilities and intelligence can be developed through effort and learning. With this mindset, we view our weaknesses as areas to improve rather than fixed limitations. A growth mindset encourages us to continuously refine our strengths and work on our weaknesses, knowing that effort leads to progress.

4. Leveraging Strengths in Professional Life

In the professional world, recognizing and embracing strengths can lead to greater career satisfaction and success. When individuals are aware of their strengths, they are better able to align their work with their natural talents and abilities, leading to higher productivity and engagement.

Employers often value employees who are self-aware and know how to leverage their strengths effectively. A professional who understands their strengths can take on projects or roles that play to their abilities, leading to increased job satisfaction and career advancement. For instance, a person who excels at problem-solving might thrive in a role that requires quick thinking and innovation, while someone with a talent for empathy and communication may excel in human resources or customer service.

In addition to benefiting individual performance, leveraging strengths in the workplace fosters collaboration and teamwork. When individuals are aware of their strengths and those of their colleagues, they can work together more efficiently, with each person contributing their best to the collective effort. This kind of collaboration leads to more creative solutions, stronger relationships, and a more positive work environment.

5. Working on Weaknesses in Professional Life

While focusing on strengths is important, addressing weaknesses is equally vital in a professional setting. Ignoring weaknesses can lead to missed opportunities, underperformance, and frustration. However, when individuals acknowledge their weaknesses and actively work on improving them, they become more well-rounded professionals.

For example, someone who struggles with time management might take a course on productivity or use time-tracking tools to become more organized. A professional who finds it difficult to delegate might seek mentorship or training on leadership skills. In doing so, individuals not only improve their performance but also increase their confidence in handling various challenges.

Additionally, acknowledging weaknesses can create a culture of openness and continuous learning in the workplace. When employees are honest about their areas of improvement, it encourages a growth-oriented mindset throughout the organization. This openness allows for constructive feedback and provides opportunities for skill development.

6. Self-Acceptance and Empowerment

Ultimately, embracing both strengths and weaknesses is a path to self-acceptance and empowerment. Self-acceptance means recognizing that we are a unique combination of talents and flaws, and that both are valuable in shaping who we are. When we accept ourselves fully, we free ourselves from the need for perfection and can focus on becoming the best version of ourselves.

Empowerment comes from knowing that our strengths give us the tools to succeed, while our weaknesses offer opportunities for growth. By embracing both, we take control of our personal development and make conscious choices about how we want to improve and evolve.

Self-acceptance also allows us to build more authentic relationships with others. When we are honest about our strengths and weaknesses, we create a space for genuine connection and mutual support. This authenticity strengthens both personal and professional relationships, leading to more meaningful interactions and collaboration.

Embracing strengths and weaknesses is a vital aspect of personal and professional growth. By recognizing and leveraging our strengths, we can achieve greater success, build confidence, and contribute to our communities. At the same time, acknowledging and working on our weaknesses allows us to grow, learn, and become more adaptable. The key to self-empowerment lies in finding a balance between the two, accepting ourselves as we are, and striving for continuous improvement. In doing so, we unlock our full potential and create a more fulfilling, balanced, and empowered life.

Developing Emotional Intelligence

Emotional intelligence (EI) refers to the ability to recognize, understand, and manage our own emotions as well as the emotions of others. It plays a crucial role in how we navigate social complexities, make decisions, and manage relationships. Unlike traditional intelligence (IQ), which is often measured by cognitive abilities and academic performance, emotional intelligence encompasses a broader range of skills, including emotional awareness, empathy, self-regulation, and social skills. Developing emotional intelligence can significantly enhance personal and professional success, improve relationships, and contribute to overall well-being.

1. Understanding Emotional Intelligence

Emotional intelligence is commonly divided into five core components:

- **Self-Awareness**: This is the ability to recognize and understand one's own emotions, strengths, weaknesses, values, and drivers. Self-awareness allows individuals to know how their emotions affect their thoughts and behavior. It also helps them understand their impact on others.
- **Self-Regulation**: This involves managing one's emotions in healthy ways, controlling impulsive feelings and behaviors, and adapting to changing circumstances. Individuals with strong self-regulation can remain calm and composed in stressful situations, allowing them to respond

thoughtfully rather than reactively.

- **Motivation**: This refers to harnessing emotions to pursue goals with energy and persistence. Emotionally intelligent individuals are often intrinsically motivated, meaning they find personal satisfaction and fulfillment in their achievements, which drives them to set and achieve challenging goals.
- **Empathy**: This is the ability to understand and share the feelings of others. Empathy involves recognizing emotional cues and responding appropriately to others' emotions, which fosters better interpersonal relationships and communication.
- **Social Skills**: This encompasses the skills needed to manage relationships effectively, including effective communication, conflict resolution, teamwork, and the ability to inspire and influence others.

Developing emotional intelligence involves enhancing these components, leading to more effective interactions and greater emotional resilience.

2. The Importance of Emotional Intelligence

The importance of emotional intelligence cannot be overstated. Research has shown that EI is a strong predictor of success in various areas of life, including professional achievement, relationship satisfaction, and mental health. Here are some key benefits of developing emotional intelligence:

- **Improved Relationships**: Individuals with high emotional intelligence are better equipped to communicate effectively, resolve conflicts, and build strong, trusting relationships. By understanding their own emotions and those of others, they can navigate social interactions more successfully, fostering collaboration and connection.
- **Better Decision-Making**: Emotional intelligence enhances decision-making by allowing individuals to consider emotions alongside rational thought. This holistic approach leads to more balanced decisions that take into account both logical reasoning and emotional factors.
- **Increased Resilience**: Emotionally intelligent individuals are better able to cope with stress, adversity, and challenges. They can manage their emotions in difficult situations, bounce back from setbacks, and maintain a positive outlook.
- **Greater Leadership Ability**: In professional settings, leaders with high emotional intelligence are more effective in motivating and inspiring

their teams. They can create a positive work environment, understand team dynamics, and foster employee engagement.

- **Enhanced Mental Well-Being**: Developing emotional intelligence can lead to greater self-awareness and self-acceptance, which contribute to improved mental health. By understanding and managing their emotions, individuals can reduce anxiety, depression, and stress.

3. Strategies for Developing Emotional Intelligence

Developing emotional intelligence is an ongoing process that requires conscious effort and practice. Here are some effective strategies to enhance each component of emotional intelligence:

a. Cultivating Self-Awareness

- **Practice Mindfulness**: Mindfulness involves paying attention to the present moment without judgment. Regular mindfulness practice, such as meditation or deep breathing exercises, can help individuals become more aware of their thoughts and emotions as they arise.
- **Reflective Journaling**: Keeping a journal allows individuals to reflect on their experiences, emotions, and reactions. Writing about daily events and feelings can provide insights into patterns of behavior and emotional responses.
- **Seek Feedback**: Asking for constructive feedback from trusted friends, family, or colleagues can help individuals gain insights into how their emotions and behaviors affect others. This external perspective can enhance self-awareness.

b. Enhancing Self-Regulation

- **Identify Triggers**: Recognizing situations or stimuli that provoke strong emotional reactions can help individuals prepare for and manage their responses. By identifying these triggers, they can develop strategies to remain calm and composed.
- **Practice Emotional Regulation Techniques**: Techniques such as deep breathing, progressive muscle relaxation, or visualization can help individuals manage their emotions in stressful situations. Engaging in physical activity or creative outlets can also serve as effective emotional release mechanisms.

- **Pause Before Reacting**: Taking a moment to pause before responding to emotionally charged situations can prevent impulsive reactions. This pause allows individuals to consider their emotions and the potential impact of their responses.

c. Fostering Motivation

- **Set Personal Goals**: Identifying meaningful goals can enhance intrinsic motivation. Setting specific, achievable goals provides direction and purpose, driving individuals to pursue their objectives with enthusiasm.
- **Celebrate Achievements**: Recognizing and celebrating small achievements along the way fosters a sense of accomplishment and motivates individuals to continue striving for their goals.
- **Cultivate a Growth Mindset**: Embracing a growth mindset—the belief that abilities and intelligence can be developed through effort—encourages individuals to persist in the face of challenges. This mindset promotes resilience and motivation.

d. Developing Empathy

- **Active Listening**: Practicing active listening involves fully focusing on the speaker, understanding their message, and responding thoughtfully. This skill fosters empathy and helps individuals connect with others on a deeper level.
- **Put Yourself in Others' Shoes**: Practicing perspective-taking can enhance empathy. By imagining how others feel in various situations, individuals can develop a better understanding of their emotions and experiences.
- **Engage in Compassionate Acts**: Volunteering or engaging in acts of kindness fosters empathy and strengthens social connections. Helping others can enhance emotional awareness and build compassion.

e. Strengthening Social Skills

- **Effective Communication**: Learning and practicing effective communication techniques, such as assertiveness and non-verbal communication, can improve interpersonal interactions. Clear and respectful communication fosters understanding and collaboration.

- **Conflict Resolution Skills**: Developing skills to navigate and resolve conflicts is essential for maintaining healthy relationships. Techniques such as active listening, negotiation, and compromise can help individuals manage disagreements constructively.
- **Building Rapport**: Engaging in social activities and building rapport with others enhances social skills. Participating in group activities or networking events can provide opportunities to practice and strengthen these skills.

4. Overcoming Challenges in Developing Emotional Intelligence

Developing emotional intelligence is a journey that can be met with challenges. Individuals may encounter obstacles such as fear of vulnerability, ingrained habits, or a lack of understanding about their emotions. Here are some strategies for overcoming these challenges:

- **Embrace Vulnerability**: Recognizing that vulnerability is a part of the emotional intelligence journey can help individuals feel more comfortable exploring their emotions. Accepting that it's okay to feel and express emotions fosters growth.
- **Practice Patience**: Developing emotional intelligence takes time and practice. Being patient with oneself during this process allows individuals to recognize that growth is gradual and that setbacks are part of the learning experience.
- **Seek Professional Support**: If individuals struggle to manage their emotions or develop emotional intelligence on their own, seeking support from a therapist or counselor can provide valuable guidance and strategies.

Developing emotional intelligence is a vital skill that significantly enhances personal and professional relationships, decision-making, and overall well-being. By cultivating self-awareness, self-regulation, motivation, empathy, and social skills, individuals can improve their emotional intelligence and navigate life's complexities more effectively. The journey toward emotional intelligence requires commitment, reflection, and practice, but the rewards—stronger relationships, greater resilience, and increased success—are well worth the effort. Embracing this journey empowers individuals to connect more deeply with themselves and others, creating a more fulfilling and meaningful life.

THREE

Cultivating Self-Love and Acceptance:

Chapter 3: Cultivating Self-Love and Acceptance:

In the journey of personal growth, cultivating self-love and acceptance serves as a vital cornerstone for emotional well-being and resilience. This chapter delves into the profound impact that self-love has on our mental health, relationships, and overall quality of life. Self-love is not merely an act of self-indulgence; it involves recognizing our intrinsic worth and treating ourselves with kindness, compassion, and respect. By embracing our imperfections and celebrating our unique qualities, we foster a healthier relationship with ourselves, allowing us to break free from the constraints of self-criticism and comparison. Acceptance plays a pivotal role in this process, as it encourages us to acknowledge our feelings and experiences without judgment, creating a safe space for growth and healing. Throughout this chapter, we will explore practical strategies for nurturing self-love, including mindfulness practices, positive affirmations, and self-care routines. By prioritizing self-love and acceptance, we empower ourselves to live authentically and cultivate a deeper sense of fulfillment and joy in our lives.

Letting Go of Perfectionism

Perfectionism is often lauded as a desirable trait, associated with high standards and an unwavering commitment to excellence. However, while striving for quality in our work and lives can be beneficial, perfectionism can also become a debilitating mindset that hinders growth, happiness, and overall well-being. Letting go of perfectionism is a crucial step toward embracing a more balanced and fulfilling life. It allows individuals to appreciate their achievements, learn from failures, and cultivate a healthier relationship with themselves and others.

Understanding Perfectionism

Perfectionism can be defined as the relentless pursuit of flawlessness and the setting of excessively high standards for oneself and others. This mindset is often accompanied by critical self-evaluations, an intense fear of failure, and an overemphasis on performance. Perfectionists may believe that their worth is directly tied to their achievements and that any imperfection is a reflection of their inadequacy. This belief can lead to a cycle of self-doubt, anxiety, and burnout, as perfectionists often find it impossible to meet their unattainable standards.

The roots of perfectionism can be deeply ingrained, stemming from various factors, including childhood experiences, societal expectations, and personality traits. Many perfectionists grew up in environments where high achievement was praised and mistakes were harshly criticized. As a result, they internalized the belief that perfection is necessary for acceptance and love. This mindset can carry into adulthood, influencing how individuals approach their careers, relationships, and personal goals.

The Costs of Perfectionism

While the desire for excellence can be motivating, the costs of perfectionism often outweigh its benefits. One of the most significant drawbacks is the fear of failure. Perfectionists may avoid taking risks or trying new things because they fear they will not meet their own expectations. This fear can lead to missed opportunities, stagnation, and a lack of personal growth.

Moreover, perfectionism can lead to chronic stress and anxiety. The pressure to perform flawlessly can be overwhelming, resulting in feelings of inadequacy and self-doubt when perfection is not achieved. This constant state of stress can contribute to various mental health issues, including anxiety disorders, depression, and burnout.

Perfectionism also negatively impacts relationships. Perfectionists may struggle to connect with others due to their high expectations, both for themselves and those around them. They may become overly critical, leading to tension and misunderstandings. Additionally, perfectionists often find it challenging to accept help or support from others, as they believe they must do everything perfectly on their own.

Letting Go of Perfectionism: A Path to Freedom

1. **Recognize Perfectionist Patterns**

The first step in letting go of perfectionism is to recognize and acknowledge the patterns that contribute to this mindset. Reflect on your beliefs about success, failure, and self-worth. Consider how these beliefs influence your thoughts, feelings, and behaviors. Journaling can be a helpful tool for identifying these patterns and gaining clarity on how perfectionism affects your life.

1. **Challenge Unrealistic Standards**

Perfectionism often thrives on unrealistic expectations. Challenge these standards by asking yourself whether they are achievable or reasonable. Instead of striving for perfection, aim for progress. Set realistic goals that allow room for mistakes and growth. Embrace the idea that "done is better than perfect." Completing a task to a satisfactory level is often more beneficial than holding out for perfection.

3. **Embrace Imperfection**

Learning to embrace imperfection is a powerful antidote to perfectionism. Accept that mistakes are a natural part of life and learning. Instead of fearing failure, view it as an opportunity for growth and development. Shift your mindset to see imperfections as valuable lessons that contribute to your journey. Practice self-compassion by treating yourself with the same kindness you would offer a friend who is struggling.

4. **Set Boundaries with Self-Criticism**

Perfectionists are often their harshest critics. Work on setting boundaries with self-criticism by becoming aware of negative self-talk and reframing it. When you notice critical thoughts arising, challenge them with more constructive and compassionate statements. For example, instead of thinking, "I'm a failure because I didn't achieve my goal," reframe it to, "I learned valuable lessons from this experience, and I can use them to improve in the future."

5. **Focus on the Process, Not Just the Outcome**

Perfectionists tend to fixate on results, leading to disappointment when expectations are not met. Shift your focus to the process of achieving your goals. Celebrate the effort and progress you make along the way, regardless of the final outcome. Engaging in the process allows you to enjoy the journey and appreciate the small victories, fostering a sense of fulfillment.

6. **Practice Mindfulness**

Mindfulness practices can help you become more aware of your thoughts and feelings, allowing you to detach from perfectionist tendencies. Techniques such as meditation, deep breathing, and body awareness can ground you in the present moment and create space for self-acceptance. By practicing mindfulness, you can develop a more balanced perspective on success and failure, reducing the grip of perfectionism.

7. **Seek Support and Connection**

Letting go of perfectionism can be challenging to navigate alone. Seek support from trusted friends, family, or a therapist who can provide encouragement and guidance. Sharing your experiences and struggles with others fosters connection and understanding. Surrounding yourself with people who appreciate you for who you are, imperfections included, can reinforce the notion that self-worth is not contingent on perfection.

8. **Engage in Self-Care**

Practicing self-care is essential in overcoming perfectionism. Prioritize activities that nurture your well-being and bring you joy. Whether it's spending time in nature, pursuing a hobby, or simply taking a break, self-care helps counterbalance the pressure to perform perfectly. Engaging in self-care fosters self-love and acceptance, reminding you that your worth is inherent, not based on achievements.

9. **Redefine Success**

Redefining your understanding of success can be transformative in letting go of perfectionism. Instead of tying success solely to outcomes, consider other factors, such as personal growth, learning, and relationships. Embrace the idea that success is not about being perfect but about being authentic and true to yourself. This shift in perspective can alleviate the pressure to achieve unattainable standards.

10. **Celebrate Your Journey**

Finally, celebrate your journey and the progress you make in letting go of perfectionism. Acknowledge the courage it takes to challenge deeply ingrained beliefs and the strength to embrace imperfection. Recognize that personal growth is a lifelong journey, and each step you take towards self-acceptance is a victory. Celebrate your achievements, no matter how small, and appreciate the unique path you are on.

Letting go of perfectionism is a liberating journey that allows individuals to embrace their true selves, imperfections and all. By recognizing perfectionist patterns, challenging unrealistic standards, and cultivating self-compassion, individuals can break free from the constraints of perfectionism. This journey fosters personal growth, enhances well-being, and strengthens relationships. Ultimately, letting go of perfectionism paves the way for a more fulfilling and authentic life, where success is defined not by flawlessness but by the richness of experience, resilience, and self-acceptance. Embracing imperfection not only brings freedom but also opens the door to creativity, connection, and a deeper appreciation for life's beautiful complexity.

Building Self-Worth

Self-worth is a fundamental aspect of our identity that significantly influences how we perceive ourselves and interact with the world around us. It encompasses the beliefs and feelings we hold about our value as individuals. Cultivating a strong sense of self-worth is essential for overall well-being, resilience, and the ability to navigate life's challenges. Unlike self-esteem, which often fluctuates based on achievements or external validation, self-worth is a deeper, intrinsic belief in one's inherent value as a person. Building self-worth is an ongoing journey that requires introspection, self-compassion, and a commitment to personal growth.

Understanding Self-Worth

Self-worth is rooted in the understanding that every individual has inherent value, regardless of their accomplishments, appearance, or societal perceptions. It is the belief that you are deserving of love, respect, and happiness simply because you exist. This foundational belief acts as a protective shield against the negativity that life may present. When you possess a strong sense of self-worth, you are less likely to be swayed by criticism, rejection, or failure. Instead, you are more resilient and capable of bouncing back from setbacks, viewing them as opportunities for growth rather than reflections of your value.

However, many individuals struggle with self-worth due to various factors, including upbringing, past experiences, and societal pressures. Negative messages from childhood, such as criticism from parents or peers, can leave lasting scars, leading to a diminished sense of self-worth. Additionally, societal expectations regarding success, beauty, and achievement can create unrealistic standards that further erode self-worth. Understanding these influences is the first step toward building a healthier sense of self.

Identifying Negative Beliefs

Building self-worth begins with recognizing and challenging negative beliefs that undermine it. Many people carry internal narratives that tell them they are not good enough, unworthy, or incapable of achieving their goals. These beliefs often stem from external influences, such as critical voices from childhood or societal standards that promote comparison and competition.

To identify these negative beliefs, it can be helpful to engage in self-reflection. Journaling is a powerful tool for this process. Write down your thoughts and feelings about yourself, paying particular attention to any negative self-talk or limiting beliefs. Ask yourself questions like: "What do I believe about my abilities?" or "How do I react to criticism?" By bringing these thoughts into conscious awareness, you can begin to challenge and reframe them.

Challenging Negative Narratives

Once you've identified negative beliefs about yourself, the next step is to challenge and reframe them. This involves questioning the validity of these beliefs and replacing them with more constructive, empowering narratives. For example, if you often think, "I'll never be successful," challenge this belief by recalling past achievements, no matter how small. Remind yourself of instances where you overcame obstacles and succeeded.

Reframing negative narratives also involves practicing self-compassion. Treat yourself with the same kindness and understanding you would offer a friend facing similar struggles. Instead of harsh self-criticism, offer gentle encouragement. Instead of saying, "I failed at that task; I'm a failure," reframe it to, "I faced a challenge, but I can learn from this experience and grow." This shift in language not only alters your perception of yourself but also fosters a more positive internal dialogue.

Setting Realistic Goals

Building self-worth involves setting and achieving realistic goals that align with your values and aspirations. Goals provide a sense of direction and purpose, helping you to cultivate confidence and a sense of accomplishment. However, it is essential to set goals that are achievable and reflective of your abilities, rather than overly ambitious or influenced by external expectations.

Begin by identifying what truly matters to you. What are your passions, interests, and values? Setting goals that resonate with your authentic self fosters a deeper connection to your worth. Break these goals into smaller, manageable steps to create a sense of progress. Celebrate each achievement, no matter how minor, as a testament to your abilities and growth. This practice not only boosts self-worth but also reinforces the belief that you are capable of achieving your aspirations.

Practicing Self-Compassion

Self-compassion is a vital component of building self-worth. It involves treating yourself with kindness, understanding, and acceptance, especially during difficult times. Rather than being overly critical or judgmental, self-compassion allows you to acknowledge your humanity and imperfections without diminishing your value.

To practice self-compassion, start by recognizing that everyone makes mistakes and experiences challenges. Instead of harshly judging yourself for setbacks, remind yourself that it's part of the human experience. Engage in positive self-talk, replacing critical thoughts with affirmations of self-worth. For instance, when faced with a setback, tell yourself, "I am doing my best, and that is enough."

Additionally, consider incorporating mindfulness practices into your routine. Mindfulness encourages present-moment awareness and helps you observe your thoughts and feelings without judgment. This practice fosters self-acceptance, allowing you to embrace your true self with compassion and kindness.

Surrounding Yourself with Positivity

The people you surround yourself with can significantly influence your self-worth. Seek relationships that uplift and support you, and distance yourself from toxic or critical individuals who undermine your sense of value. Surrounding yourself with positive influences fosters an environment where self-worth can flourish.

Engage with friends, family, and mentors who encourage your growth and celebrate your achievements. Their support can reinforce your sense of worth and provide valuable perspective during challenging times. Additionally, consider joining communities or groups that align with your interests and values, fostering connections with like-minded individuals who share your passions.

Embracing Vulnerability

Embracing vulnerability is a powerful step in building self-worth. Vulnerability involves being open and honest about your feelings, experiences, and insecurities. It allows you to connect with others on a deeper level and fosters authentic relationships.

When you embrace vulnerability, you recognize that it's okay to be imperfect and that seeking help or support is a sign of strength, not weakness. Share your thoughts and feelings with trusted individuals, allowing them to offer support and understanding. This openness creates a safe space for growth and reinforces the belief that you are worthy of love and acceptance.

Celebrating Your Unique Qualities

Each individual possesses unique qualities, strengths, and talents that contribute to their sense of self-worth. Take time to reflect on what makes you unique. What are your strengths? What qualities do you admire in yourself? Acknowledging and celebrating these attributes fosters a deeper appreciation for your value as an individual.

Consider creating a list of your positive qualities and achievements. This list serves as a reminder of your worth, especially during moments of self-doubt. Regularly revisit this list to reinforce the belief that you are deserving of love and respect.

The Ongoing Journey of Building Self-Worth

Building self-worth is not a one-time achievement; it is an ongoing journey that requires continuous effort and self-reflection. Life is full of ups and downs, and external circumstances may challenge your sense of worth. However, by actively engaging in practices that reinforce your value, you can cultivate a resilient and lasting sense of self-worth.

Regularly check in with yourself, reflecting on your thoughts, beliefs, and feelings. Adjust your practices as needed, incorporating new strategies that resonate with your evolving self. Remember that self-worth is not contingent on external validation but is rooted in your inherent value as a person.

Building self-worth is a transformative process that empowers individuals to recognize their inherent value and embrace their authentic selves. By challenging negative beliefs, setting realistic goals, practicing self-compassion, and surrounding ourselves with positivity, we can cultivate a strong sense of self-worth that withstands life's challenges. This journey involves celebrating our unique qualities, embracing vulnerability, and committing to ongoing growth. Ultimately, building self-worth fosters resilience, enhances well-being, and enables us to live more fulfilling lives, grounded in the understanding that we are deserving of love, respect, and happiness simply because we exist.

The Role of Self-Care in Personal Growth

Self-care is often viewed as a luxury, a mere indulgence reserved for those with ample time and resources. However, it is a crucial component of personal growth that plays a transformative role in our overall well-being. At its core, self-care encompasses the practices and activities that nurture our physical, emotional, and mental health. By prioritizing self-care, individuals can create a strong foundation for personal growth, resilience, and fulfillment.

Understanding Self-Care

Self-care is not simply about pampering oneself; it is an intentional practice that acknowledges the need for balance in our lives. It involves recognizing and addressing our needs in various areas, including physical health, emotional well-being, and mental clarity. While self-care looks different for everyone, its essence lies in fostering a positive relationship with oneself and promoting a sense of well-being.

In recent years, the importance of self-care has gained significant recognition, especially in the context of fast-paced lifestyles and the rising prevalence of stress and burnout. The demands of work, family, and societal expectations can lead to neglecting our own needs, resulting in exhaustion and dissatisfaction. By integrating self-care into our daily routines, we can combat these challenges and enhance our personal growth.

The Connection Between Self-Care and Personal Growth

1. **Enhanced Physical Health**

Physical well-being is the foundation of personal growth. When we engage in self-care practices that promote physical health, we set ourselves up for success in other areas of life. This includes regular exercise, a balanced diet, sufficient sleep, and proper hydration. Prioritizing physical health not only boosts our energy levels but also improves our mood and cognitive function.

Exercise, for example, releases endorphins, the body's natural mood elevators, which can help combat feelings of anxiety and depression. A healthy diet fuels our bodies, providing the nutrients necessary for optimal functioning. By taking care of our physical health, we create a solid base from which personal growth can flourish.

2. **Emotional Resilience**

Self-care is integral to building emotional resilience, which is crucial for navigating life's challenges. Engaging in self-care activities allows individuals to process their emotions, reduce stress, and foster a sense of calm. Practices such as mindfulness, journaling, and meditation can help individuals develop greater self-awareness, enabling them to understand and manage their emotions more effectively.

Moreover, self-care encourages individuals to set healthy boundaries, which are essential for maintaining emotional well-being. By learning to say no and prioritizing our needs, we can protect ourselves from emotional exhaustion and cultivate a supportive environment conducive to personal growth.

3. **Improved Mental Clarity**

Mental well-being is closely tied to personal growth, and self-care plays a pivotal role in maintaining a clear and focused mind. Engaging in activities that promote mental clarity, such as reading, engaging in creative pursuits, or practicing mindfulness, can enhance cognitive function and overall mental health.

Taking breaks from daily responsibilities is also crucial for mental clarity. Whether it's stepping away from work for a few minutes or scheduling a day off to recharge, these moments of respite allow our minds to reset and rejuvenate. When we give ourselves the space to think and reflect, we become more receptive to new ideas and perspectives, facilitating personal growth.

4. **Fostering Self-Compassion**

Self-care is an expression of self-compassion, a fundamental aspect of personal growth. Many individuals struggle with self-criticism, holding themselves to unattainable standards. Engaging in self-care practices cultivates a sense of kindness toward oneself, allowing individuals to recognize their inherent worth and value.

Self-compassion involves treating oneself with the same understanding and support that one would offer a friend in times of struggle. By incorporating self-care into our lives, we create opportunities for self-forgiveness and acceptance. This shift in mindset fosters resilience, enabling individuals to learn from their mistakes and embrace their imperfections as part of the growth journey.

5. **Nurturing Personal Interests and Passions**

Self-care is an opportunity to reconnect with our interests and passions, which is essential for personal growth. Many individuals become so absorbed in their responsibilities that they neglect the activities that bring them joy and fulfillment. Carving out time for hobbies, creative pursuits, or simply indulging in interests can ignite a sense of purpose and creativity.

Whether it's painting, gardening, writing, or engaging in a sport, nurturing these interests allows individuals to express themselves authentically and explore their unique talents. Engaging in activities we love promotes a sense of accomplishment and satisfaction, further propelling our personal growth.

6. **Building Healthy Relationships**

Self-care extends beyond the individual; it influences our relationships with others. When we prioritize our own well-being, we become better equipped to nurture and maintain healthy relationships. Engaging in self-care fosters emotional stability, enabling individuals to approach relationships with empathy, understanding, and patience.

Furthermore, taking care of ourselves allows us to establish boundaries that protect our energy and mental health. Healthy relationships thrive on mutual respect and understanding, and by modeling self-care, we encourage those around us to prioritize their own well-being as well.

7. **Cultivating Mindfulness and Presence**

Mindfulness is a key aspect of self-care that significantly contributes to personal growth. By practicing mindfulness, individuals can cultivate a greater awareness of their thoughts, feelings, and experiences. This awareness fosters a deeper understanding of oneself and the ability to navigate life's challenges with clarity and purpose.

Engaging in mindfulness practices, such as meditation or deep breathing exercises, allows individuals to become more present in their daily lives. This presence enhances decision-making, reduces stress, and fosters a sense of gratitude for the moment. By cultivating mindfulness, individuals can create a solid foundation for personal growth.

8. **Creating a Personalized Self-Care Routine**

To fully realize the benefits of self-care, it is essential to create a personalized self-care routine that aligns with individual needs and preferences. This routine should encompass various aspects of well-being, including physical, emotional, mental, and social dimensions.

Begin by assessing your current self-care practices and identifying areas for improvement. Consider incorporating activities that resonate with you, whether it's setting aside time for exercise, practicing gratitude, or engaging in creative pursuits. It's important to remember that self-care is not a one-size-fits-all approach; what works for one person may not resonate with another.

Overcoming Barriers to Self-Care

Despite the importance of self-care, many individuals face barriers that hinder their ability to prioritize it. Common obstacles include time constraints, guilt, and societal pressures. Overcoming these barriers requires a shift in mindset and the recognition that self-care is not selfish; it is a necessary investment in one's overall well-being.

Start by scheduling self-care activities as you would any other commitment. Block off time in your calendar for exercise, relaxation, or hobbies. Allow yourself to embrace the idea that taking care of yourself is essential for your ability to care for others. Practice self-compassion by recognizing that you deserve moments of rest and rejuvenation.

The role of self-care in personal growth is invaluable. By prioritizing self-care, individuals create a strong foundation for physical, emotional, and mental well-being. This intentional practice fosters resilience, self-compassion, and improved relationships, all of which are essential for personal growth. As we navigate the complexities of life, embracing self-care allows us to reconnect with ourselves, nurture our passions, and cultivate a greater sense of fulfillment. Ultimately, self-care is not just an indulgence; it is a vital aspect of personal growth that empowers us to thrive in all areas of our lives. By integrating self-care into our daily routines, we can embark on a transformative journey toward a more balanced, authentic, and fulfilling existence.

The Role of Self-Care in Personal Growth

Self-care is often viewed as a luxury, a mere indulgence reserved for those with ample time and resources. However, it is a crucial component of personal growth that plays a transformative role in our overall well-being. At its core, self-care encompasses the practices and activities that nurture our physical, emotional, and mental health. By prioritizing self-care, individuals can create a strong foundation for personal growth, resilience, and fulfillment.

Understanding Self-Care

Self-care is not simply about pampering oneself; it is an intentional practice that acknowledges the need for balance in our lives. It involves recognizing and addressing our needs in various areas, including physical health, emotional well-being, and mental clarity. While self-care looks different for everyone, its essence lies in fostering a positive relationship with oneself and promoting a sense of well-being.

In recent years, the importance of self-care has gained significant recognition, especially in the context of fast-paced lifestyles and the rising prevalence of stress and burnout. The demands of work, family, and societal expectations can lead to neglecting our own needs, resulting in exhaustion and dissatisfaction. By integrating self-care into our daily routines, we can combat these challenges and enhance our personal growth.

The Connection Between Self-Care and Personal Growth

1. **Enhanced Physical Health**

Physical well-being is the foundation of personal growth. When we engage in self-care practices that promote physical health, we set ourselves up for success in other areas of life. This includes regular exercise, a balanced diet, sufficient sleep, and proper hydration. Prioritizing physical health not only boosts our energy levels but also improves our mood and cognitive function.

Exercise, for example, releases endorphins, the body's natural mood elevators, which can help combat feelings of anxiety and depression. A healthy diet fuels our bodies, providing the nutrients necessary for optimal functioning. By taking care of our physical health, we create a solid base from which personal growth can flourish.

2. **Emotional Resilience**

Self-care is integral to building emotional resilience, which is crucial for navigating life's challenges. Engaging in self-care activities allows individuals to process their emotions, reduce stress, and foster a sense of calm. Practices such as mindfulness, journaling, and meditation can help individuals develop greater self-awareness, enabling them to understand and manage their emotions more effectively.

Moreover, self-care encourages individuals to set healthy boundaries, which are essential for maintaining emotional well-being. By learning to say no and prioritizing our needs, we can protect ourselves from emotional exhaustion and cultivate a supportive environment conducive to personal growth.

3. **Improved Mental Clarity**

Mental well-being is closely tied to personal growth, and self-care plays a pivotal role in maintaining a clear and focused mind. Engaging in activities that promote mental clarity, such as reading, engaging in creative pursuits, or practicing mindfulness, can enhance cognitive function and overall mental health.

Taking breaks from daily responsibilities is also crucial for mental clarity. Whether it's stepping away from work for a few minutes or scheduling a day off to recharge, these moments of respite allow our minds to reset and rejuvenate. When we give ourselves the space to think and reflect, we become more receptive to new ideas and perspectives, facilitating personal growth.

4. **Fostering Self-Compassion**

Self-care is an expression of self-compassion, a fundamental aspect of personal growth. Many individuals struggle with self-criticism, holding themselves to unattainable standards. Engaging in self-care practices cultivates a sense of kindness toward oneself, allowing individuals to recognize their inherent worth and value.

Self-compassion involves treating oneself with the same understanding and support that one would offer a friend in times of struggle. By incorporating self-care into our lives, we create opportunities for self-forgiveness and acceptance. This shift in mindset fosters resilience, enabling individuals to learn from their mistakes and embrace their imperfections as part of the growth journey.

5. **Nurturing Personal Interests and Passions**

Self-care is an opportunity to reconnect with our interests and passions, which is essential for personal growth. Many individuals become so absorbed in their responsibilities that they neglect the activities that bring them joy and fulfillment. Carving out time for hobbies, creative pursuits, or simply indulging in interests can ignite a sense of purpose and creativity.

Whether it's painting, gardening, writing, or engaging in a sport, nurturing these interests allows individuals to express themselves authentically and explore their unique talents. Engaging in activities we love promotes a sense of accomplishment and satisfaction, further propelling our personal growth.

6. **Building Healthy Relationships**

Self-care extends beyond the individual; it influences our relationships with others. When we prioritize our own well-being, we become better equipped to nurture and maintain healthy relationships. Engaging in self-care fosters emotional stability, enabling individuals to approach relationships with empathy, understanding, and patience.

Furthermore, taking care of ourselves allows us to establish boundaries that protect our energy and mental health. Healthy relationships thrive on mutual respect and understanding, and by modeling self-care, we encourage those around us to prioritize their own well-being as well.

7. **Cultivating Mindfulness and Presence**

Mindfulness is a key aspect of self-care that significantly contributes to personal growth. By practicing mindfulness, individuals can cultivate a greater awareness of their thoughts, feelings, and experiences. This awareness fosters a deeper understanding of oneself and the ability to navigate life's challenges with clarity and purpose.

Engaging in mindfulness practices, such as meditation or deep breathing exercises, allows individuals to become more present in their daily lives. This presence enhances decision-making, reduces stress, and fosters a sense of gratitude for the moment. By cultivating mindfulness, individuals can create a solid foundation for personal growth.

8. **Creating a Personalized Self-Care Routine**

To fully realize the benefits of self-care, it is essential to create a personalized self-care routine that aligns with individual needs and preferences. This routine should encompass various aspects of well-being, including physical, emotional, mental, and social dimensions.

Begin by assessing your current self-care practices and identifying areas for improvement. Consider incorporating activities that resonate with you, whether it's setting aside time for exercise, practicing gratitude, or engaging in creative pursuits. It's important to remember that self-care is not a one-size-fits-all approach; what works for one person may not resonate with another.

Overcoming Barriers to Self-Care

Despite the importance of self-care, many individuals face barriers that hinder their ability to prioritize it. Common obstacles include time constraints, guilt, and societal pressures. Overcoming these barriers requires a shift in mindset and the recognition that self-care is not selfish; it is a necessary investment in one's overall well-being.

Start by scheduling self-care activities as you would any other commitment. Block off time in your calendar for exercise, relaxation, or hobbies. Allow yourself to embrace the idea that taking care of yourself is essential for your ability to care for others. Practice self-compassion by recognizing that you deserve moments of rest and rejuvenation.

The role of self-care in personal growth is invaluable. By prioritizing self-care, individuals create a strong foundation for physical, emotional, and mental well-being. This intentional practice fosters resilience, self-compassion, and improved relationships, all of which are essential for personal growth. As we navigate the complexities of life, embracing self-care allows us to reconnect with ourselves, nurture our passions, and cultivate a greater sense of fulfillment. Ultimately, self-care is not just an indulgence; it is a vital aspect of personal growth that empowers us to thrive in all areas of our lives. By integrating self-care into our daily routines, we can embark on a transformative journey toward a more balanced, authentic, and fulfilling existence.

FOUR

Lessons on Relationships

Part II: Lessons on Relationships

In the intricate tapestry of human existence, relationships serve as both the foundation and the framework that shape our experiences, emotions, and growth. Part II: Lessons on Relationships delves into the multifaceted dynamics that define our interactions with others, offering profound insights into the nature of connection, communication, and empathy. Understanding relationships requires us to explore not only how we relate to others but also how our interactions reflect our inner selves. This section emphasizes the importance of nurturing healthy connections, fostering effective communication, and cultivating empathy as essential tools for personal growth. Through the exploration of different relationship types—be it familial, romantic, or friendships—we uncover the lessons that teach us about love, respect, trust, and compromise. Ultimately, the quality of our relationships significantly influences our well-being and happiness, making it essential to learn and grow from our interactions with others. As we embark on this journey through the lessons of relationships, we are reminded that every connection, whether joyful or challenging, offers valuable insights that contribute to our personal evolution.

Chapter 4: The Art of Communication

Listening with Empathy

Listening with empathy is an essential skill that fosters deeper connections, enhances understanding, and cultivates a supportive environment in our interactions with others. It involves not just hearing the words spoken but also understanding the emotions and intentions behind those words. When we listen empathetically, we create a safe space for others to express their thoughts and feelings, allowing for more meaningful conversations and relationships.

Empathy is the ability to put ourselves in someone else's shoes, to feel what they are feeling, and to understand their perspective. It goes beyond sympathy, which often involves feeling pity or sorrow for someone else's situation. Instead, empathetic listening requires active engagement and an openness to genuinely understand another person's experience. This practice encourages individuals to communicate more freely and honestly, knowing they will be heard and valued.

To effectively listen with empathy, one must first develop strong active listening skills. This includes maintaining eye contact, using affirming gestures, and refraining from interrupting while the other person speaks. Active listening also requires focusing on the speaker's words, tone, and body language, which can provide invaluable context to their message. By demonstrating attentiveness, we signal to the speaker that their thoughts and feelings matter, fostering an atmosphere of trust and openness.

An important aspect of empathetic listening is the ability to reflect back what we hear. This involves paraphrasing or summarizing the speaker's main points, which not only clarifies understanding but also shows that we are genuinely engaged in the conversation. For instance, saying, "It sounds like you're feeling overwhelmed by your workload," not only validates the speaker's feelings but also encourages them to share more. Reflective listening helps to deepen the dialogue and allows the speaker to explore their emotions further.

It's also crucial to be mindful of our own biases and assumptions while listening empathetically. Preconceived notions can cloud our understanding and hinder our ability to connect with others. Instead of jumping to conclusions or offering unsolicited advice, we should approach conversations with curiosity and an open heart. By doing so, we allow the speaker to express themselves fully without fear of judgment or dismissal.

Additionally, silence can be a powerful tool in empathetic listening. Allowing for pauses in the conversation gives the speaker space to gather their thoughts and encourages deeper reflection. It also communicates patience and respect for their feelings, reinforcing the idea that their experiences are valued.

Listening with empathy can have a profound impact on our relationships, both personally and professionally. In personal relationships, it helps to build intimacy and trust, enabling individuals to feel comfortable sharing their vulnerabilities. In professional settings, empathetic listening fosters collaboration and enhances teamwork, as colleagues feel more respected and understood.

Furthermore, practicing empathetic listening can contribute to our own personal growth. By engaging with diverse perspectives, we expand our understanding of the world and develop greater compassion for others. This skill not only improves our interpersonal relationships but also enriches our own emotional intelligence.

In conclusion, listening with empathy is a vital skill that enhances communication and strengthens relationships. By actively engaging in empathetic listening, we create a supportive environment where individuals feel valued and understood. This practice fosters deeper connections, encourages open dialogue, and contributes to our growth as compassionate individuals. In a world that often prioritizes speed and efficiency over genuine connection, the ability to listen empathetically stands out as a powerful tool for creating lasting, meaningful relationships. Embracing this skill not only enriches our interactions with others but also transforms the way we experience the world around us Speaking with Intention

Navigating Difficult Conversations

Difficult conversations are an inevitable part of life, whether they occur in personal relationships, professional settings, or even casual interactions. These discussions often involve sensitive topics, conflicting viewpoints, or emotions that can lead to tension and discomfort. Mastering the art of navigating difficult conversations is essential for effective communication and can significantly enhance our relationships, foster understanding, and promote resolution.

Understanding the Importance of Difficult Conversations

At first glance, avoiding difficult conversations may seem appealing. However, shying away from such discussions often leads to unresolved issues, lingering resentment, and misunderstandings. Engaging in open dialogue about tough topics, on the other hand, allows individuals to express their feelings, clarify intentions, and work toward solutions. These conversations can lead to growth and stronger connections, even if they are initially uncomfortable.

Preparing for the Conversation

Preparation is key to successfully navigating difficult conversations. Start by clearly defining the issue at hand and identifying your objectives.

What do you hope to achieve by engaging in this conversation? Whether it's resolving a conflict, expressing concerns, or seeking clarity, having a clear purpose will guide your approach.

Next, consider the other person's perspective. Anticipating their reactions and feelings can help you approach the conversation with empathy and understanding. Think about how your message may be received and prepare to address their concerns or emotions.

Choosing the right time and place is also crucial. Select a setting that is private and conducive to open dialogue. Avoid bringing up sensitive topics in the heat of the moment or in public spaces where distractions may hinder effective communication. By creating a safe environment, both parties are more likely to feel comfortable expressing their thoughts and feelings.

Active Listening

During difficult conversations, active listening is paramount. This involves fully focusing on the speaker, understanding their message, and responding thoughtfully. Practice reflective listening by paraphrasing what the other person has said, which demonstrates that you are engaged and value their perspective.

For example, if a colleague expresses frustration about workload distribution, you might say, "It sounds like you're feeling overwhelmed and would like to discuss how tasks are divided." This response not only acknowledges their feelings but also opens the door for further dialogue.

Avoid interrupting or formulating your response while the other person is speaking. Instead, give them the space to express themselves fully. This will encourage a more productive conversation and demonstrate your respect for their viewpoint.

Managing Emotions

Difficult conversations can evoke strong emotions, both for you and the other person involved. It's essential to remain aware of your emotions and manage them effectively throughout the discussion. If you feel yourself becoming defensive or upset, take a moment to breathe and ground yourself before responding.

Recognize the emotional undertones in the conversation, both your own and those of the other person. If the other person appears upset, acknowledge their feelings without becoming defensive. For instance, you might say, "I can see that this topic is really affecting you, and I want to understand your perspective better."

Establishing a tone of compassion and understanding can help diffuse tension and create an environment where both parties feel safe to express their emotions. The goal is not to win an argument but to engage in a constructive conversation that leads to resolution.

Finding Common Ground

During difficult conversations, it's essential to identify common ground. Acknowledging shared values or goals can help create a collaborative atmosphere. For instance, if you're discussing a disagreement with a partner about finances, focus on your mutual desire for stability and security.

Finding common ground can facilitate compromise and solution-finding. When both parties recognize that they are working toward a shared objective, it becomes easier to navigate differences and arrive at a resolution that satisfies everyone involved.

Emphasizing Solutions

As the conversation progresses, shift the focus toward finding solutions. Instead of dwelling on problems, encourage brainstorming to generate potential resolutions. This collaborative approach fosters a sense of teamwork and reinforces the idea that both parties are invested in resolving the issue.

Ask open-ended questions to facilitate dialogue about solutions. For instance, "What do you think would help us manage our workload more effectively?" This question invites the other person to contribute ideas, promoting a sense of agency and involvement in the problem-solving process.

Be open to feedback and remain flexible in your approach. Sometimes, the solution may require compromise or adapting to new ideas. This willingness to collaborate strengthens relationships and builds trust.

Following Up

After the difficult conversation, take the time to reflect on the discussion. Consider what went well and what could be improved for future conversations. This self-reflection can enhance your communication skills and prepare you for similar discussions in the future.

If resolutions were reached, it's essential to follow up and ensure that both parties are adhering to the agreed-upon solutions. Check in with the other person to assess how they are feeling and whether the situation has improved. This ongoing dialogue demonstrates commitment and reinforces the positive outcomes of the conversation.

Navigating difficult conversations is a crucial skill that can significantly impact our personal and professional lives. By preparing thoughtfully, actively listening, managing emotions, finding common ground, emphasizing solutions, and following up, we can transform uncomfortable discussions into opportunities for growth and understanding. While these conversations may never be easy, embracing the challenge can lead to stronger relationships, enhanced communication, and a deeper appreciation for diverse perspectives. Ultimately, it is through these conversations that we learn, evolve, and foster meaningful connections with others.

FIVE

BUILDING AND NURTURING RELATIONSHIPS

Building and Nurturing Relationships delves into the foundational elements essential for cultivating meaningful connections in our personal and professional lives. Relationships are not merely formed; they require ongoing effort, understanding, and compassion to thrive. This chapter explores the significance of trust, communication, and mutual respect as the cornerstones of strong relationships. It emphasizes the importance of active listening and empathetic engagement, which allow individuals to connect on a deeper level and address conflicts constructively. Additionally, the chapter highlights the role of vulnerability in fostering intimacy and openness, encouraging readers to embrace their authentic selves. Through practical strategies and insights, readers will learn how to nurture existing relationships and build new ones, ultimately enriching their lives and creating a supportive network that enhances personal growth and well-being. By understanding that relationships are a dynamic interplay of give and take, this chapter encourages a proactive approach to cultivating connections that stand the test of time.

The Foundation of Trust

Trust serves as the cornerstone of all meaningful relationships, whether they exist in personal, professional, or community contexts. It is an intricate and delicate bond that takes time to establish but can be easily damaged or lost. Understanding the foundational elements of trust is essential for building and nurturing relationships that are resilient, genuine, and fulfilling.

What is Trust?

At its core, trust is the belief in the reliability, integrity, and competence of another person or entity. It involves a willingness to be vulnerable, as trusting someone means putting oneself at risk of disappointment or betrayal. However, trust also fosters security, encouraging open communication, collaboration, and emotional safety.

Trust is built through consistent actions and behaviors over time. When individuals demonstrate honesty, transparency, and accountability, they create a framework for trust to develop. Conversely, inconsistency, dishonesty, or lack of follow-through can erode trust, often leading to conflict and misunderstanding.

Elements of Trust

Several key elements contribute to the foundation of trust.

1. **Reliability:** One of the most critical aspects of trust is reliability. When someone consistently meets commitments and follows through on promises, they signal to others that they can be depended upon. This reliability cultivates confidence in the relationship, allowing individuals to feel secure in their interactions.
2. **Honesty:** Honesty is fundamental to establishing trust. When individuals communicate openly and truthfully, they create a sense of authenticity that fosters deeper connections. Being candid about thoughts, feelings, and intentions helps clarify expectations and prevents misunderstandings.
3. **Transparency:** Transparency involves being open about motives and decisions. When individuals are transparent, they provide insight into their thought processes and actions, making it easier for others to understand their perspectives. This openness can mitigate suspicion and foster trust, especially in challenging situations.
4. **Competence:** Trust is also influenced by an individual's perceived competence. When people demonstrate expertise, skill, and knowledge in their actions, they inspire confidence in their abilities. This competence reassures others that they can rely on them to make sound judgments and decisions.
5. **Empathy:** Empathy plays a crucial role in trust-building. When individuals show genuine care and concern for the feelings and

experiences of others, it fosters emotional connections that enhance trust. Empathetic communication allows individuals to feel valued and understood, reinforcing their belief in the integrity of the relationship.

Building Trust

Building trust takes time and intentionality. It begins with self-awareness and self-reflection, as individuals must understand their values, strengths, and areas for growth. Establishing trust within oneself is crucial, as individuals who trust themselves are more likely to extend that trust to others.

Engaging in open and honest communication is vital for cultivating trust. Practicing active listening—giving undivided attention and responding thoughtfully—demonstrates respect and validation for the other person's thoughts and feelings. Creating a safe environment for sharing opinions and concerns encourages others to be vulnerable, fostering deeper connections.

Moreover, consistency in behavior is essential for maintaining trust. When individuals act in alignment with their words, it reinforces the belief that they are dependable and trustworthy. Conversely, inconsistency can lead to doubt and uncertainty, undermining the foundation of trust.

Repairing Trust

While trust is vital, it is not infallible. Mistakes, misunderstandings, and conflicts can lead to breaches of trust. However, repairing trust is possible and often necessary for the relationship to move forward. Acknowledging mistakes, taking responsibility, and expressing genuine remorse are crucial steps in the repair process.

Rebuilding trust requires open communication about the breach and a commitment to making amends. This may involve reassessing boundaries, clarifying expectations, and demonstrating through consistent actions that trust can be re-established.

Conclusion

The foundation of trust is integral to creating and sustaining meaningful relationships. By embodying the key elements of reliability, honesty, transparency, competence, and empathy, individuals can cultivate a strong framework of trust that fosters emotional safety and mutual respect. Trust is a dynamic process, requiring ongoing effort and intention. However, the rewards of establishing and nurturing trust are immeasurable, as they lead to deeper connections, enhanced collaboration, and a greater sense of belonging in both personal and professional contexts. Embracing trust as a fundamental principle can transform relationships, empowering individuals to navigate the complexities of life with confidence and resilience.

Maintaining Healthy Boundaries

Establishing and maintaining healthy boundaries is essential for nurturing relationships, promoting self-respect, and ensuring emotional well-being. Boundaries define where one person ends and another begins, creating a space where individuals can interact while respecting each other's needs, feelings, and limits. Understanding how to set and maintain boundaries is crucial for personal development and the health of all types of relationships, whether they are familial, romantic, or professional.

Understanding Boundaries

Boundaries can be physical, emotional, or psychological. Physical boundaries pertain to personal space and physical touch, while emotional boundaries relate to how we share our feelings and who we allow into our emotional lives. Psychological boundaries define how we think and what we allow others to influence. Recognizing and understanding these different types of boundaries is the first step toward establishing healthy ones.

Healthy boundaries are not walls meant to keep people out; rather, they are guidelines that foster respect and understanding. They enable individuals to express their needs and desires while also acknowledging those of others. When boundaries are respected, relationships can thrive, leading to mutual trust and healthy communication.

The Importance of Boundaries

Establishing boundaries is vital for several reasons. First and foremost, boundaries promote self-care. They help individuals protect their emotional and physical well-being by ensuring that they do not overextend themselves or compromise their values. This self-care is essential for maintaining mental health and avoiding burnout, especially in demanding environments like workplaces or caregiving roles.

Additionally, boundaries foster healthy relationships. When individuals communicate their limits and respect those of others, it creates a safe space for open dialogue and honest interactions. This practice can reduce conflict, prevent resentment, and encourage mutual support. Healthy boundaries also allow individuals to maintain their individuality and autonomy, ensuring that they do not lose themselves in their relationships.

Setting Boundaries

Setting boundaries begins with self-reflection. Individuals must first identify their needs, values, and limits. Consider the following questions:

1. What are my emotional triggers?
2. What situations make me feel uncomfortable or overwhelmed?
3. How much time and energy do I want to invest in my relationships?

By answering these questions, individuals can gain insight into the boundaries they need to establish. Once identified, it's crucial to communicate these boundaries clearly and assertively. Effective communication is key to ensuring that others understand your limits.

When discussing boundaries, use "I" statements to express your feelings without sounding accusatory. For example, instead of saying, "You always interrupt me," try, "I feel frustrated when I am interrupted during conversations." This approach encourages open dialogue and reduces defensiveness.

Maintaining Boundaries

Once boundaries are set, it is essential to maintain them. Consistency is crucial; if boundaries are allowed to be crossed occasionally, it can create confusion and resentment. Here are some strategies for maintaining healthy boundaries:

1. **Be Assertive:** Assertiveness involves expressing your needs confidently and respectfully. When someone crosses your boundaries, address it immediately and reinforce your limits. This may involve saying, "I need some time alone right now," or "I cannot take on more responsibilities at work."
2. **Practice Self-Care:** Regularly assess your emotional and physical state to ensure that your boundaries are serving your well-being. If you find yourself feeling overwhelmed, reevaluate your commitments and make adjustments as needed. Prioritizing self-care ensures that you have the energy to maintain healthy boundaries.
3. **Be Prepared for Pushback:** Some individuals may resist your boundaries, particularly if they are used to a different dynamic. Stay firm and remember that it is your right to establish limits. If someone continues to disregard your boundaries, consider whether the relationship is worth maintaining.

4. **Seek Support:** Surround yourself with individuals who respect your boundaries and encourage your growth. Whether it's friends, family, or a therapist, having a support system can help reinforce your commitment to maintaining healthy boundaries.

Flexibility and Adaptation

While consistency is vital, it's also important to recognize that boundaries can evolve. Life circumstances, personal growth, and changes in relationships may necessitate adjustments to boundaries. Regularly check in with yourself and others to assess whether your boundaries still serve your needs.

Being open to revising boundaries can also strengthen relationships. It demonstrates that you are engaged and willing to adapt to the needs of both yourself and others. However, any changes should be communicated clearly to ensure mutual understanding.

The Benefits of Healthy Boundaries

Maintaining healthy boundaries leads to numerous benefits, including improved self-esteem, better communication, and enhanced relationship satisfaction. When individuals honor their limits and those of others, it creates an atmosphere of respect and understanding. This positive environment fosters deeper connections and encourages individuals to express themselves authentically.

Moreover, healthy boundaries can reduce stress and anxiety. When people know their limits and communicate them effectively, they are less likely to feel overwhelmed or taken advantage of. This clarity allows for more balanced interactions and empowers individuals to prioritize their well-being.

Maintaining healthy boundaries is essential for personal growth, emotional well-being, and nurturing meaningful relationships. By understanding the importance of boundaries, setting clear limits, and consistently reinforcing them, individuals can create a supportive environment where mutual respect and open communication thrive. Boundaries are not barriers; they are vital tools that promote self-care and foster healthy connections. Embracing the practice of setting and maintaining boundaries can lead to a more fulfilling, balanced, and authentic life. Ultimately, healthy boundaries empower individuals to live with intention, respect their needs, and build relationships that enrich their lives.

The Role of Forgiveness in Healing

Forgiveness is often viewed as a personal virtue or moral obligation, but its significance extends far beyond these dimensions. It is a powerful catalyst for healing, both for individuals and relationships, and plays a crucial role in emotional well-being. Understanding the role of forgiveness in the healing process can provide profound insights into how individuals can overcome pain, resentment, and emotional turmoil, paving the way for a healthier, more fulfilling life.

Understanding Forgiveness

At its core, forgiveness involves a conscious decision to let go of resentment and thoughts of revenge against someone who has caused harm. It does not necessarily mean excusing the behavior or reconciling with the offender; rather, it is about freeing oneself from the burden of negative emotions. Forgiveness is often misconstrued as a sign of weakness or submission, but in reality, it requires immense strength and courage. It is an act of self-liberation that allows individuals to reclaim their power over their emotions and experiences.

Forgiveness can be both a personal journey and a relational process. On an individual level, it involves introspection and a commitment to healing. In a relational context, it may involve reconciling with others, though this is not always necessary for forgiveness to take place. Understanding these nuances is essential for appreciating the depth of forgiveness as a healing tool.

The Emotional Burden of Holding onto Grudges

When individuals hold onto grudges, they often find themselves trapped in a cycle of negative emotions. Resentment, anger, and bitterness can take a toll on mental and physical health. Studies have shown that prolonged resentment can lead to increased stress, anxiety, and even depression. The emotional burden of these feelings can manifest in physical symptoms, including fatigue, headaches, and weakened immune responses.

Furthermore, holding onto grudges can disrupt personal relationships. It creates a barrier that hinders communication, intimacy, and trust. The emotional energy spent on harboring resentment could be better utilized in nurturing relationships and personal growth. Ultimately, the cost of not forgiving can be significant, impacting not only the individual but also those around them.

The Healing Power of Forgiveness

Forgiveness is a transformative process that can lead to profound healing. It allows individuals to release the emotional weight of past grievances, opening the door to peace and acceptance. Here are several key ways in which forgiveness contributes to healing:

1. **Emotional Release:** The act of forgiving provides an emotional release, alleviating feelings of anger and resentment. This release can lead to a sense of relief and lightness, allowing individuals to move forward without the burden of negative emotions weighing them down.
2. **Restoration of Inner Peace:** Forgiveness fosters a sense of inner peace. When individuals let go of grudges, they often find that their minds are less cluttered with painful memories and thoughts. This mental clarity can create space for positive emotions, including joy, gratitude, and hope.
3. **Improved Mental Health:** Numerous studies have linked forgiveness with improved mental health outcomes. Individuals who practice forgiveness report lower levels of anxiety and depression, as well as increased emotional well-being. By releasing negative emotions, individuals can cultivate a more positive outlook on life.
4. **Enhanced Relationships:** Forgiveness can repair and strengthen relationships. When individuals choose to forgive, they often create opportunities for open communication and rebuilding trust. This process can lead to deeper connections and healthier interactions, benefiting both parties involved.
5. **Personal Growth:** The journey of forgiveness often prompts self-reflection and personal growth. Individuals may gain insights into their values, triggers, and emotional responses. This awareness can lead to greater emotional intelligence and resilience, empowering individuals to navigate future challenges with a healthier mindset.

The Process of Forgiveness

Forgiveness is not a one-time event; it is a process that unfolds over time. Here are several steps individuals can take to navigate their forgiveness journey:

1. **Acknowledge the Pain:** The first step in forgiveness is acknowledging the pain caused by the offense. It's essential to recognize and validate one's feelings of hurt, anger, and betrayal. Suppressing these emotions can hinder the forgiveness process.

2. **Reflect on the Impact:** Understanding the impact of the offense on one's life can help individuals gain perspective. This reflection allows individuals to assess how holding onto resentment affects their well-being and relationships.
3. **Make a Conscious Choice:** Forgiveness is ultimately a choice. Individuals must decide to let go of resentment and pursue healing. This decision may involve affirming that forgiveness is for oneself, not for the offender.
4. **Communicate, if Appropriate:** In some cases, it may be beneficial to communicate with the person who caused the harm. This conversation can provide an opportunity for clarification, accountability, and healing. However, this step is not always necessary for forgiveness to occur.
5. **Practice Self-Compassion:** Forgiveness is often accompanied by self-compassion. Individuals should be gentle with themselves as they navigate their emotions and experiences. Recognizing that healing is a journey can alleviate pressure and promote a sense of patience.
6. **Let Go of Expectations:** Forgiveness may not lead to reconciliation or a change in the other person's behavior. Letting go of expectations regarding the outcome can free individuals from disappointment and allow them to focus on their healing.

Forgiveness in Different Contexts

Forgiveness can manifest differently across various contexts, including familial, romantic, and professional relationships. Each context presents unique challenges and opportunities for forgiveness.

In familial relationships, long-standing grievances may require deeper exploration, as family dynamics can complicate the forgiveness process. Romantic relationships often involve intense emotions, making forgiveness both a challenge and a vital component of healing. In professional settings, forgiveness can facilitate collaboration and productivity, especially in environments where conflicts may arise.

The role of forgiveness in healing cannot be overstated. It is a powerful tool that enables individuals to release emotional burdens, restore inner peace, and enhance relationships. By understanding the transformative nature of forgiveness and navigating its process with intention and compassion, individuals can foster personal growth and resilience. Ultimately, forgiveness is not just about absolving others; it is a gift to oneself—an essential step toward healing, growth, and emotional freedom. Embracing forgiveness allows individuals to reclaim their power, paving the way for a healthier, more fulfilling life.

SIX

LOVE AND COMPASSION

Love and Compassion delves into the profound connection between these two fundamental aspects of the human experience. Love, in its myriad forms—romantic, familial, platonic, and self-love—serves as a powerful force that fosters connection and understanding among individuals. Compassion, on the other hand, is the ability to empathize with the suffering of others and respond with kindness and support. This chapter explores how love and compassion intersect, highlighting their significance in promoting emotional well-being and healing. By cultivating a compassionate mindset, individuals can not only enhance their relationships but also contribute to a more empathetic and harmonious world. Through practical strategies and insights, readers will learn how to express love and compassion in their daily lives, transforming their interactions and nurturing a sense of belonging and community. Ultimately, this chapter emphasizes that love and compassion are not just feelings but active choices that can lead to profound personal and collective growth.

Understanding Love Beyond Romance

Love is a multifaceted emotion that extends far beyond the boundaries of romantic relationships. While romance often receives significant attention in literature, media, and everyday conversations, the various forms of love that exist in our lives deserve equal recognition and understanding. This broader perspective of love encompasses familial bonds, friendships, self-love, and altruistic love, each contributing uniquely to our overall well-being and sense of connection.

The Many Facets of Love

1. **Familial Love**: Familial love is often one of the first types of love we experience. This form of love encompasses the affection and bonds shared between family members, including parents, siblings, and extended relatives. Familial love is characterized by loyalty, support, and a deep-rooted sense of belonging. It provides individuals with a secure foundation, fostering emotional growth and resilience. Despite its unconditional nature, familial love can also be complex, as familial ties may come with expectations and responsibilities. Understanding this dynamic can help individuals navigate the challenges that arise within family relationships while still appreciating the deep connections formed through shared history and experiences.
2. **Friendship**: Friendship is another vital aspect of love that significantly contributes to our emotional well-being. Friends offer companionship, understanding, and support, creating a sense of community that enriches our lives. Unlike familial love, which may sometimes feel obligatory, friendships are typically built on mutual interests, respect, and affection. They allow individuals to express their true selves without fear of judgment. Friendships can also act as a source of emotional support during challenging times, providing a safe space for vulnerability and connection. The importance of nurturing these relationships cannot be overstated, as friends often become a chosen family, playing a crucial role in our journey through life.
3. **Self-Love**: Self-love is an essential yet often overlooked form of love that involves recognizing one's worth, embracing one's flaws, and prioritizing personal well-being. In a society that frequently emphasizes external validation, cultivating self-love can be a challenging endeavor. However, it is vital for overall mental and emotional health. Self-love enables individuals to set healthy boundaries, practice self-care, and develop a positive self-image. It serves as the foundation for all other forms of love, as one cannot genuinely love others without first loving oneself. Understanding and embracing self-love fosters resilience and empowers individuals to navigate life's challenges with confidence and grace.
4. **Altruistic Love**: Altruistic love, or love for humanity, transcends individual relationships and embodies a profound concern for the well-being of others. This form of love drives individuals to engage in acts of kindness, compassion, and service, fostering a sense of interconnectedness within communities and the world at large. Altruistic love can manifest in various ways, from volunteering and

charitable work to advocating for social justice and environmental sustainability. By understanding the importance of altruistic love, individuals can contribute positively to society, creating a ripple effect that encourages others to engage in acts of kindness and compassion. This collective effort can lead to a more empathetic and harmonious world, reminding us that love is a powerful force for change.

The Interconnectedness of Love

While it is essential to understand the different forms of love, it is equally important to recognize their interconnectedness. Familial love, friendship, self-love, and altruistic love are not mutually exclusive; they often overlap and influence one another. For instance, self-love can enhance the quality of friendships and familial relationships by fostering healthier boundaries and more authentic connections. Conversely, strong friendships can reinforce self-love, providing support and encouragement that nurtures personal growth.

In romantic relationships, understanding these various forms of love can also lead to healthier dynamics. A romantic partnership built on a foundation of friendship, mutual respect, and self-love is more likely to thrive than one based solely on physical attraction or societal expectations. By recognizing and valuing the different dimensions of love, individuals can cultivate richer, more fulfilling relationships.

Love and Emotional Well-Being

Understanding love beyond romance has profound implications for emotional well-being. The diverse expressions of love contribute significantly to overall happiness, fulfillment, and resilience. Research has shown that strong social connections, including friendships and familial bonds, are linked to lower levels of stress, anxiety, and depression. These relationships provide a support system that helps individuals navigate life's challenges, promoting emotional stability.

Moreover, cultivating self-love and altruistic love can enhance emotional resilience. When individuals prioritize their well-being and engage in acts of kindness toward others, they create a positive feedback loop that reinforces their sense of self-worth and connectedness. This interconnectedness fosters a sense of belonging, helping individuals feel valued and understood in their communities.

Practical Steps for Embracing Love Beyond Romance

1. **Nurture Friendships**: Take the time to invest in friendships by reaching out, making plans, and being present. Engage in meaningful conversations and show appreciation for your friends. This intentionality can strengthen bonds and deepen connections.
2. **Practice Self-Love**: Incorporate self-care practices into your daily routine. This can include setting aside time for hobbies, engaging in physical activity, practicing mindfulness, and being gentle with yourself during challenging times. Prioritizing self-love fosters a positive self-image and resilience.
3. **Strengthen Family Bonds**: Make an effort to connect with family members, whether through regular communication, shared activities, or quality time. Recognize the unique qualities that each family member brings to your life and express gratitude for their presence.
4. **Engage in Altruism**: Seek out opportunities to help others in your community. Volunteering, supporting local initiatives, or simply performing random acts of kindness can foster a sense of connection and purpose. Altruistic love enriches both the giver and the receiver, creating a cycle of positivity.
5. **Cultivate Empathy**: Practice empathy by actively listening to others and seeking to understand their perspectives. This skill can enhance friendships, familial relationships, and altruistic love by promoting deeper connections and emotional support.

Understanding love beyond romance enriches our lives and fosters emotional well-being. By acknowledging the various forms of love—familial, friendship, self-love, and altruistic love—we can cultivate deeper connections, enhance our emotional resilience, and contribute positively to our communities. Embracing this broader perspective on love allows individuals to experience a more fulfilling and meaningful existence, reminding us that love, in all its forms, is a powerful force that shapes our lives and the world around us. Ultimately, recognizing and nurturing these diverse expressions of love can lead to personal growth, stronger relationships, and a greater sense of connection to humanity as a whole

The Power of Compassion in Relationships

Compassion is a powerful force that shapes the dynamics of human relationships, fostering understanding, empathy, and connection. It is the ability to recognize the suffering of others and take action to alleviate that suffering, whether through kind words, supportive gestures, or active listening. In a world often filled with stress and conflict, compassion serves as a vital balm that not only heals individual wounds but also strengthens the bonds between people. Understanding the power of compassion in relationships can lead to deeper connections, improved communication, and a greater sense of community.

The Essence of Compassion

At its core, compassion goes beyond mere sympathy or empathy. While sympathy involves feeling pity for someone's situation and empathy requires putting oneself in another's shoes, compassion takes it a step further by motivating individuals to act to help alleviate suffering. This active response is what makes compassion transformative in relationships. It encourages a sense of shared humanity, allowing individuals to connect on a deeper emotional level.

Compassion is not limited to romantic relationships; it plays an essential role in familial, platonic, and even professional relationships. In each context, the application of compassion can lead to enhanced emotional well-being and stronger relational bonds. When individuals practice compassion, they create an environment where others feel valued, understood, and supported.

The Impact of Compassion on Relationships

1. **Strengthening Emotional Bonds**: Compassion fosters emotional intimacy and trust in relationships. When individuals show genuine concern for one another's well-being, they build a foundation of trust that allows for vulnerability. This vulnerability is crucial for developing deeper connections. Sharing personal struggles and feelings can be daunting, but when compassion is present, individuals feel safe to open up, knowing their emotions will be met with understanding and support.
2. **Improved Communication**: Compassion enhances communication in relationships. When individuals approach conversations with a compassionate mindset, they are more likely to listen actively and respond thoughtfully. This creates an atmosphere where both parties feel heard and respected. Compassionate communication encourages honesty and openness, reducing misunderstandings and fostering more productive discussions. In contrast, when compassion is absent, communication can become strained, leading to conflicts and emotional distance.

3. **Conflict Resolution**: Every relationship will encounter challenges and conflicts. Compassion plays a crucial role in resolving these disputes. When individuals approach conflicts with compassion, they are more likely to seek solutions that prioritize the feelings and needs of all parties involved. This approach shifts the focus from winning an argument to finding common ground, allowing for constructive dialogue and compromise. Compassionate individuals are better equipped to manage their emotions and respond to conflict with patience, empathy, and understanding, which ultimately leads to healthier resolutions.
4. **Fostering Forgiveness**: Compassion is integral to the process of forgiveness. When someone has been hurt or wronged, it can be challenging to move past the pain without understanding the underlying reasons for the behavior. Compassion allows individuals to view the situation from the perspective of the other person, fostering a sense of understanding that can facilitate forgiveness. Recognizing that everyone is fallible and capable of making mistakes creates space for healing and restoration in relationships.
5. **Promoting Well-Being**: Compassionate relationships have a profound impact on mental and emotional well-being. Studies have shown that individuals in compassionate relationships experience lower levels of stress, anxiety, and depression. The support and understanding provided by compassionate partners, friends, or family members contribute to a greater sense of security and happiness. Additionally, compassion has been linked to increased resilience, enabling individuals to cope more effectively with life's challenges.

Cultivating Compassion in Relationships

While the benefits of compassion in relationships are clear, cultivating this quality requires intentional effort and practice. Here are several strategies for fostering compassion in your relationships:

1. **Practice Active Listening**: One of the most powerful ways to show compassion is through active listening. This involves giving your full attention to the speaker, maintaining eye contact, and avoiding distractions. Instead of formulating your response while the other person is speaking, focus on understanding their perspective and emotions. Reflect back what you hear to ensure clarity and validate their feelings.

2. **Express Empathy**: Empathy is a crucial component of compassion. Take the time to acknowledge the feelings of others, even if you cannot fully relate to their experiences. Use empathetic language, such as "I can only imagine how difficult this must be for you" or "It's understandable that you feel this way." By expressing empathy, you demonstrate that you care about their emotional experience.
3. **Engage in Kind Acts**: Small acts of kindness can significantly impact the compassionate nature of a relationship. Offer support during challenging times, whether through a simple gesture like cooking a meal, lending a listening ear, or helping with daily tasks. These acts convey that you are invested in the well-being of the other person and reinforce your emotional bond.
4. **Practice Self-Compassion**: Compassion for others begins with self-compassion. It's essential to treat yourself with the same kindness and understanding that you offer to others. Acknowledge your own struggles and be gentle with yourself when faced with challenges. When you cultivate self-compassion, you are better equipped to extend compassion to those around you.
5. **Reflect on Your Reactions**: During conflicts or challenging interactions, take a moment to reflect on your emotional reactions. Are you responding with judgment or frustration? Consider how you would feel if you were in the other person's position. This practice can help you approach situations with a more compassionate mindset.
6. **Encourage Vulnerability**: Create a safe space for vulnerability in your relationships. Encourage open communication by sharing your feelings, thoughts, and experiences. When you model vulnerability, it invites others to do the same, fostering deeper connections and compassion.

The Broader Implications of Compassion

The power of compassion in relationships extends beyond personal interactions; it has broader implications for society as a whole. In a world often marked by division and conflict, fostering compassion can lead to greater social cohesion and understanding. When individuals practice compassion in their relationships, they contribute to a culture of empathy that can ripple out into communities and beyond.

Compassionate relationships encourage individuals to engage with and support one another, creating a sense of belonging and interconnectedness. This sense of community is crucial in addressing societal challenges, as compassionate individuals are more likely to advocate for social justice, equality, and positive change. By nurturing compassion in personal relationships, individuals can play a role in building a more compassionate society.

The power of compassion in relationships is undeniable. It strengthens emotional bonds, improves communication, aids in conflict resolution, promotes well-being, and fosters forgiveness. By cultivating compassion, individuals can create deeper, more meaningful connections with others, enhancing their emotional health and overall quality of life. As we strive to practice compassion in our relationships, we not only enrich our lives but also contribute to a more empathetic and harmonious world. In embracing compassion, we unlock the potential for profound transformation, both within ourselves and in the relationships we cherish.

Creating Deeper Connections through Vulnerability

Vulnerability is often perceived as a weakness, an opening to hurt or betrayal, yet it is, in fact, one of the most powerful tools for building genuine connections with others. When we allow ourselves to be vulnerable, we reveal our true selves, complete with our fears, insecurities, and imperfections. This openness can foster deeper relationships by cultivating trust, empathy, and intimacy. In a world that often prioritizes strength and self-sufficiency, embracing vulnerability can transform not only how we relate to others but also how we understand ourselves.

The Nature of Vulnerability

Vulnerability involves exposing our innermost feelings, thoughts, and fears, often in the face of uncertainty. It is about being honest with ourselves and others, recognizing that we are all imperfect beings navigating life's complexities. Brené Brown, a researcher and expert on vulnerability, defines it as "uncertainty, risk, and emotional exposure." The essence of vulnerability lies in its authenticity; it allows us to break free from the facades we often maintain to protect ourselves from judgment or rejection.

In relationships, vulnerability can manifest in various forms—sharing personal experiences, expressing emotions, admitting mistakes, or asking for help. These acts of openness create an opportunity for others to respond with empathy and understanding, laying the groundwork for a stronger emotional connection.

The Importance of Vulnerability in Relationships

1. **Building Trust**: Trust is a fundamental component of any meaningful relationship. When we are vulnerable, we signal to others that we trust them enough to share our innermost thoughts and feelings. This mutual exchange of vulnerability fosters a safe space where both parties can express themselves freely. Trust grows when individuals witness each other's authentic selves, reinforcing the belief that they can rely on one another.
2. **Encouraging Empathy**: Vulnerability invites empathy. When we open up about our struggles and experiences, we allow others to see our humanity. This encourages them to reflect on their own experiences, creating a shared understanding. Empathy thrives in an environment where individuals feel safe to express their emotions, leading to deeper connections. When we empathize with one another, we move beyond superficial interactions and create bonds that resonate on a deeper level.
3. **Fostering Intimacy**: Emotional intimacy is essential for healthy relationships, and vulnerability is a key ingredient in its cultivation. When we share our fears, dreams, and insecurities, we create a space for intimacy to flourish. This depth of connection allows individuals to support one another in meaningful ways, enhancing the overall quality of the relationship. Intimacy is not solely about physical closeness; it is rooted in emotional connection, and vulnerability is the pathway to achieving that closeness.
4. **Reducing Fear of Judgment**: One of the greatest barriers to vulnerability is the fear of judgment or rejection. However, when individuals embrace vulnerability, they create an atmosphere where judgment is less likely. By modeling openness, they encourage others to reciprocate, breaking down walls that often separate individuals. When people feel accepted for who they are, it reduces the anxiety associated with vulnerability, making it easier to share thoughts and feelings.
5. **Enhancing Authenticity**: Authenticity is about being true to oneself, and vulnerability is a crucial aspect of that journey. When we allow ourselves to be vulnerable, we shed the masks we often wear to conform to societal expectations. This authenticity not only strengthens our self-identity but also attracts like-minded individuals who appreciate us for who we truly are. Authentic relationships are built on the foundation of vulnerability, where individuals can fully express themselves without fear of being judged.

The Challenges of Embracing Vulnerability

While the benefits of vulnerability are clear, it is not without its challenges. Many people struggle to embrace vulnerability due to past experiences, fear of rejection, or societal pressures to appear strong and self-sufficient. Here are some common challenges individuals may face when attempting to be vulnerable:

1. **Fear of Rejection**: The fear of being rejected or ridiculed can be paralyzing. This fear often stems from previous experiences of being hurt or judged, leading individuals to build emotional walls as a defense mechanism. Overcoming this fear requires a conscious effort to recognize that vulnerability is a strength, not a weakness.
2. **Cultural Conditioning**: Many cultures prioritize stoicism and self-reliance, teaching individuals to suppress their emotions and vulnerabilities. This conditioning can create internal conflicts, making it challenging to embrace vulnerability. Acknowledging and challenging these cultural norms is essential for personal growth and deeper connections.
3. **Past Trauma**: Individuals who have experienced trauma may find it particularly difficult to be vulnerable. Past hurts can create a reluctance to trust others, leading to avoidance of emotional openness. Healing from trauma often involves a journey of self-discovery and support, enabling individuals to gradually embrace vulnerability in relationships.
4. **Misunderstanding Vulnerability**: Some individuals may equate vulnerability with weakness, viewing it as a flaw to be avoided. This misunderstanding can prevent them from experiencing the depth of connection that vulnerability offers. Educating oneself about the true nature of vulnerability is crucial in overcoming these misconceptions.

Strategies for Embracing Vulnerability

1. **Start Small**: Begin by sharing minor vulnerabilities with trusted friends or family members. This could involve expressing a fear, sharing a personal goal, or discussing a challenge. Starting small allows you to build confidence and gradually expand your comfort zone.
2. **Practice Active Listening**: When others share their vulnerabilities with you, practice active listening. Respond with empathy and validation, showing that you appreciate their openness. This not only strengthens

your relationship but also encourages them to be more vulnerable in the future.

3. **Create a Safe Space**: Foster an environment where vulnerability is welcomed and encouraged. This can involve setting aside time for meaningful conversations or engaging in activities that promote connection. When individuals feel safe, they are more likely to open up.
4. **Challenge Negative Self-Talk**: Pay attention to your inner dialogue when considering being vulnerable. Challenge any negative thoughts that arise, reminding yourself of the benefits of vulnerability and the strength it brings to relationships. Replace self-criticism with self-compassion, recognizing that everyone has flaws and insecurities.
5. **Reflect on Your Experiences**: Take time to reflect on your past experiences with vulnerability. Consider moments when being open led to deeper connections and emotional growth. These reflections can reinforce the positive aspects of vulnerability and motivate you to continue embracing it.

The Transformative Power of Vulnerability

Embracing vulnerability is not merely about sharing personal struggles; it is a transformative process that reshapes how we interact with ourselves and others. By allowing ourselves to be vulnerable, we open the door to deeper connections, enhanced emotional intimacy, and authentic relationships. Vulnerability has the power to dissolve barriers, fostering trust and empathy that enrich our lives.

As we navigate a world that often emphasizes strength and self-reliance, it is essential to recognize that vulnerability is not a liability but a strength. It is an invitation to connect, to share, and to grow together. When we embrace vulnerability, we create a tapestry of relationships woven with understanding, compassion, and authenticity. Ultimately, vulnerability is a journey—a journey that leads us to deeper connections and a more profound understanding of ourselves and those around us.

SEVEN

Lessons on Resilience and Adversity

Part III: Lessons on Resilience and Adversity

In the journey of life, resilience and adversity are two inseparable companions that teach us invaluable lessons about strength, perseverance, and the human spirit. Adversity can come in many forms—personal challenges, loss, failure, or unexpected changes—and while it may test our limits, it also serves as a powerful catalyst for growth and self-discovery. Through facing difficult times, we learn to adapt, develop coping mechanisms, and ultimately emerge stronger than before. Resilience is not merely about bouncing back from hardship; it is about embracing the lessons learned along the way, fostering a mindset that views obstacles as opportunities for development. This section delves into the significance of resilience, highlighting how our responses to adversity shape our character, inform our values, and enhance our capacity for empathy and compassion. By cultivating resilience, we not only navigate life's challenges with greater ease but also inspire those around us to harness their strength in the face of adversity.

Chapter 7: Embracing Change and Uncertainty

Learning to Adapt in Difficult Times

Life is often a series of unexpected events and challenges that test our ability to cope and adapt. Whether faced with personal loss, economic hardship, or health crises, learning to adapt in difficult times is a crucial skill that can determine our resilience and overall well-being. Adaptability involves more than simply adjusting to changes; it encompasses a mindset of flexibility, problem-solving, and growth. It is about embracing uncertainty and finding ways to thrive despite adversity.

Understanding Adaptability

Adaptability refers to the ability to adjust to new conditions, environments, or situations. It is a fundamental aspect of human behavior and a key trait that contributes to personal resilience. When we encounter difficult times, our initial reactions may include fear, anger, or sadness. However, the ability to adapt allows us to move beyond these initial emotions and find ways to cope with the challenges we face.

Adaptability is not a fixed trait; it can be developed and strengthened over time. By learning to adapt, we cultivate a sense of agency over our lives, empowering ourselves to navigate obstacles with confidence and determination. This skill is particularly vital in today's fast-paced and ever-changing world, where the ability to pivot and respond to unexpected circumstances has become increasingly important.

The Importance of Learning to Adapt

1. **Resilience Building**: Adaptability is closely linked to resilience—the capacity to recover from difficulties. Each time we adapt to a challenging situation, we build our resilience muscles. We learn that we can overcome obstacles and that setbacks are not the end but rather part of a larger journey. This resilience helps us face future challenges with a greater sense of strength and confidence.
2. **Problem-Solving Skills**: Learning to adapt in difficult times enhances our problem-solving abilities. When confronted with challenges, we are forced to think critically and creatively about potential solutions. This problem-solving mindset can lead to innovative approaches and new perspectives that may not have emerged in more stable times.
3. **Emotional Intelligence**: Adaptability fosters emotional intelligence, which is the ability to understand and manage our own emotions as well as empathize with others. As we navigate difficult situations, we become more aware of our emotional responses and those of others, allowing us to connect on a deeper level. This emotional awareness can improve our relationships and communication skills.
4. **Growth Mindset**: Adapting to challenges encourages a growth mindset—the belief that our abilities and intelligence can be developed

through effort and learning. When we view difficulties as opportunities for growth, we are more likely to embrace challenges rather than shy away from them. This mindset allows us to see failures as stepping stones to success rather than as insurmountable obstacles.

5. **Enhanced Coping Strategies**: Learning to adapt involves developing coping strategies that help us manage stress and uncertainty. These strategies can include mindfulness practices, seeking support from others, or reframing negative thoughts. By building a toolkit of coping mechanisms, we can approach difficult situations with a greater sense of control and resilience.

Strategies for Learning to Adapt

1. **Embrace Change**: One of the first steps in learning to adapt is to embrace change rather than resist it. Change is an inevitable part of life, and accepting that reality can make it easier to navigate difficult times. Acknowledging that change is a natural process allows us to shift our perspective and focus on what we can control.
2. **Cultivate a Support System**: Building and maintaining a strong support system is essential for adapting to difficult situations. Surrounding ourselves with supportive friends, family, or community members provides us with a safety net during challenging times. When we share our experiences and feelings with others, we often gain new insights and encouragement, making it easier to navigate adversity.
3. **Practice Mindfulness**: Mindfulness involves being present in the moment and acknowledging our thoughts and feelings without judgment. This practice can help us become more aware of our emotional responses to difficult situations, allowing us to respond thoughtfully rather than react impulsively. Mindfulness can also reduce anxiety and stress, making it easier to adapt to changes.
4. **Set Realistic Goals**: In times of difficulty, it can be helpful to set small, achievable goals that allow us to regain a sense of control. These goals can serve as stepping stones toward larger objectives and help us focus on progress rather than perfection. By breaking down challenges into manageable tasks, we can build momentum and foster a sense of accomplishment.
5. **Be Open to Learning**: Each difficult situation presents an opportunity for learning and growth. Maintaining a curious mindset allows us to

explore new ways of thinking and problem-solving. When faced with challenges, ask yourself what lessons can be learned and how you can apply those lessons moving forward. This approach fosters resilience and adaptability.

6. **Develop Flexibility**: Flexibility is a key component of adaptability. Being open to new ideas and willing to adjust our plans can make it easier to navigate change. Practice letting go of rigid expectations and embracing the idea that there may be multiple paths to achieving your goals. Flexibility allows us to pivot when necessary and find alternative solutions.
7. **Reflect on Past Experiences**: Reflecting on previous challenges can provide valuable insights into how we have successfully adapted in the past. Consider moments when you faced adversity and how you navigated those situations. Identifying the strategies that worked for you can empower you to apply similar approaches in the face of new challenges.
8. **Practice Self-Compassion**: Learning to adapt in difficult times can be emotionally taxing, and it's important to be gentle with ourselves during this process. Practice self-compassion by acknowledging your feelings and recognizing that it's okay to struggle. Treat yourself with the same kindness and understanding that you would offer to a friend facing a similar situation.

Real-Life Examples of Adaptability

The power of adaptability can be illustrated through various real-life examples. For instance, consider the story of a small business owner who faced significant financial challenges during an economic downturn. Rather than giving up, they adapted their business model by pivoting to online sales and exploring new markets. This willingness to change not only helped them survive the crisis but also led to new opportunities and growth.

Similarly, individuals who have faced personal adversity—such as illness or loss—often find ways to adapt that lead to profound personal growth. A person diagnosed with a chronic illness may learn to advocate for themselves and develop new coping strategies, ultimately leading to a deeper understanding of their own resilience and a desire to help others in similar situations.

Learning to adapt in difficult times is an essential skill that can enhance our resilience and overall well-being. By embracing change, cultivating a support system, practicing mindfulness, and developing flexibility, we can navigate challenges with greater ease and confidence. Adaptability not only empowers us to overcome obstacles but also fosters personal growth and deeper connections with others. In a world filled with uncertainty, the ability to adapt becomes a crucial asset, enabling us to thrive despite adversity. Ultimately, the lessons learned through adaptation can shape our character, inform our values, and inspire others to embrace their own capacity for resilience. As we face the inevitable ups and downs of life, let us remember that each challenge is an opportunity for growth and transformation.

The Growth Mindset: Unlocking Potential Through Belief and Resilience

The concept of a growth mindset has gained significant traction in educational, professional, and personal development circles. Coined by psychologist Carol Dweck, the term describes the belief that abilities and intelligence can be developed through dedication, hard work, and perseverance. This perspective contrasts sharply with a fixed mindset, where individuals believe their talents and intelligence are static traits that cannot be changed. Understanding and embracing a growth mindset can lead to transformative changes in our approach to challenges, learning, and personal growth.

Understanding the Growth Mindset

At its core, the growth mindset is based on the belief that effort, learning, and resilience are key components of success. Individuals with a growth mindset view challenges as opportunities for growth rather than obstacles to avoid. They understand that failure is not a reflection of their abilities but rather a stepping stone toward improvement. This mindset encourages individuals to take risks, learn from their mistakes, and seek feedback as a means of enhancing their skills.

Dweck's research indicates that the way we perceive our abilities can significantly impact our performance and achievements. For instance, students with a growth mindset tend to embrace challenges, persist in the face of setbacks, and ultimately achieve higher levels of success compared to their counterparts with a fixed mindset. This is because they are more likely to see effort as a pathway to mastery rather than a futile endeavor.

The Benefits of a Growth Mindset

1. **Increased Resilience**: One of the most significant benefits of a growth mindset is the development of resilience. Individuals with this mindset are more likely to bounce back from setbacks and continue striving toward their goals. They view obstacles as temporary and surmountable, which enables them to maintain motivation even in the face of difficulties.
2. **Enhanced Learning**: A growth mindset fosters a love for learning and self-improvement. Individuals become more curious and eager to explore new ideas and concepts. This intrinsic motivation to learn leads to deeper understanding and mastery of subjects, as they are willing to invest time and effort into their growth.
3. **Greater Achievement**: Those who embrace a growth mindset often experience higher levels of achievement. By believing in the power of effort and persistence, they are more likely to set challenging goals and pursue them with determination. Research shows that students with a growth mindset tend to achieve better grades and perform better in various academic settings.
4. **Improved Relationships**: A growth mindset can enhance interpersonal relationships by fostering a culture of support and encouragement. Individuals who believe in growth are more likely to provide constructive feedback and celebrate others' successes. This collaborative approach creates a positive environment that nurtures growth for everyone involved.
5. **Reduced Fear of Failure**: Individuals with a growth mindset are less fearful of failure, as they understand that it is an essential part of the learning process. This perspective encourages them to take risks and try new things, ultimately leading to personal and professional growth.

Developing a Growth Mindset

While some people may naturally gravitate toward a growth mindset, it is a skill that can be cultivated over time. Here are several strategies to help foster a growth mindset in yourself and others:

1. **Embrace Challenges**: Instead of shying away from challenges, seek them out. Embracing difficult tasks can help you build resilience and develop new skills. When faced with a challenge, remind yourself that it is an opportunity to learn and grow.

2. **Reframe Failure**: Change your perspective on failure. Instead of viewing it as a setback, see it as a valuable learning experience. Analyze what went wrong, identify areas for improvement, and apply those lessons moving forward.
3. **Cultivate Curiosity**: Foster a sense of curiosity about the world around you. Ask questions, seek new experiences, and challenge yourself to learn something new regularly. This approach can ignite your passion for learning and encourage a growth-oriented mindset.
4. **Set Learning Goals**: Focus on setting goals that emphasize learning rather than just performance. For example, instead of aiming for a specific grade, set a goal to master a particular skill or concept. This shift in focus encourages a process-oriented approach that values growth over outcomes.
5. **Seek Feedback**: Actively seek constructive feedback from others. This can provide valuable insights into your strengths and areas for improvement. Embrace feedback as a tool for growth rather than criticism.
6. **Surround Yourself with Growth-Oriented Individuals**: Engage with people who share a growth mindset. Their positive attitudes and encouragement can inspire you to adopt a similar outlook. Participate in discussions, collaborate on projects, and celebrate each other's successes.
7. **Practice Self-Compassion**: Be kind to yourself when facing setbacks. Acknowledge your efforts and remind yourself that growth is a journey. Practicing self-compassion allows you to bounce back from difficulties and maintain motivation.

The Role of Language in Shaping Mindset

The language we use plays a significant role in shaping our mindset. Dweck emphasizes the importance of "growth language" when discussing abilities and achievements. For example, instead of saying, "I'm not good at math," try saying, "I'm learning to improve my math skills." This subtle shift in language reinforces the idea that improvement is possible and encourages a growth mindset.

Parents, educators, and leaders can also influence mindset through their language. Encouraging phrases like "You worked hard" or "I can see how much effort you put in" emphasize the importance of effort and perseverance. Conversely, labeling someone as "talented" or "smart" can inadvertently promote a fixed mindset, as it suggests that these traits are innate and unchangeable.

The Impact of a Growth Mindset in Education and Beyond

In educational settings, promoting a growth mindset has shown to enhance student engagement and achievement. Teachers who foster this mindset create an environment where students feel safe to take risks and make mistakes. This approach encourages collaboration, critical thinking, and a lifelong love of learning.

Beyond education, a growth mindset can significantly impact personal and professional development. In the workplace, organizations that cultivate a growth mindset culture encourage employees to innovate, collaborate, and take ownership of their development. This culture not only boosts employee morale but also drives organizational success.

Challenges to Cultivating a Growth Mindset

Despite the numerous benefits of a growth mindset, several challenges can impede its development:

1. **Cultural Influences**: Societal norms and cultural values may promote a fixed mindset, emphasizing talent and innate ability over effort and learning. Overcoming these cultural influences requires conscious effort and awareness.
2. **Fear of Judgment**: Many individuals fear judgment from others, leading them to avoid challenges or risk-taking. This fear can be paralyzing and hinder the development of a growth mindset.
3. **Past Experiences**: Negative past experiences can create barriers to adopting a growth mindset. Individuals who have faced repeated failures may struggle to believe in their ability to improve.
4. **Fixed Mindset Triggers**: Certain situations or environments may trigger fixed mindset thinking, making it difficult to maintain a growth perspective. Recognizing these triggers and actively working to reframe thoughts can help mitigate their impact.

The growth mindset is a powerful concept that can transform the way we approach challenges, learning, and personal development. By embracing the belief that our abilities can be developed through effort and perseverance, we open ourselves up to new possibilities and opportunities for growth. Cultivating a growth mindset requires intentional practice and a willingness to embrace challenges, learn from failures, and seek feedback. As we develop this mindset, we build resilience, enhance our problem-solving skills, and ultimately unlock our full potential. In a world that constantly changes and presents new challenges, the growth mindset serves as a guiding principle, empowering us to thrive in the face of adversity and become the best versions of ourselves.

Finding Strength in Vulnerability

Vulnerability is often perceived as a weakness in our society, synonymous with fear, uncertainty, and emotional exposure. Many people go to great lengths to shield themselves from vulnerability, believing it makes them susceptible to harm or judgment. However, a growing body of research and personal testimonies highlights that vulnerability is, in fact, a source of strength and resilience. Embracing vulnerability can lead to deeper connections, personal growth, and an enhanced sense of authenticity. This essay explores the concept of vulnerability, its misconceptions, and how finding strength in vulnerability can transform our lives and relationships.

Understanding Vulnerability

Vulnerability can be defined as the willingness to show up and be seen, even when there are no guarantees of a positive outcome. It involves opening ourselves to emotional risk and uncertainty, whether in our personal lives, professional settings, or relationships. Dr. Brené Brown, a prominent researcher in the field of vulnerability, defines it as "uncertainty, risk, and emotional exposure." Her research has shown that vulnerability is the birthplace of creativity, innovation, and change, and it is a crucial component of meaningful connections.

Understanding vulnerability begins with acknowledging that everyone experiences it in various forms. Whether it's sharing our fears, admitting our mistakes, or expressing our true feelings, vulnerability is a universal aspect of the human experience. By recognizing that we all face moments of vulnerability, we can begin to dismantle the stigma surrounding it.

Misconceptions About Vulnerability

1. **Vulnerability Equals Weakness**: One of the most common misconceptions is that vulnerability equates to weakness. Many people believe that displaying vulnerability makes them appear fragile or incapable. However, embracing vulnerability takes immense courage and strength. It requires a deep understanding of oneself and the willingness to face the possibility of rejection or failure.

2. **Vulnerability Is a Choice**: While we may choose how and when to express our vulnerability, the experience of vulnerability is often involuntary. Life presents situations where we are forced to confront our fears, insecurities, and uncertainties. Recognizing that vulnerability is a natural part of the human experience can help us reframe our perspective on it.
3. **Vulnerability Is a One-Time Event**: Some people believe that vulnerability is a one-time act, such as sharing a personal story or emotion. In reality, vulnerability is an ongoing process that requires continual self-awareness and openness. It involves consistently showing up for ourselves and others, even when it feels uncomfortable.
4. **Vulnerability Leads to Shame**: While vulnerability can lead to feelings of shame if met with judgment or rejection, it can also foster deeper connections and understanding. When we share our vulnerabilities with others, we often find that they respond with empathy and support, creating a space for healing and growth.

The Strength Found in Vulnerability

1. **Deeper Connections**: Embracing vulnerability can lead to more profound and authentic connections with others. When we share our fears, struggles, and insecurities, we invite others to do the same. This mutual sharing fosters trust and intimacy, allowing relationships to flourish. Vulnerable conversations can transform superficial interactions into meaningful connections that enrich our lives.
2. **Personal Growth**: Vulnerability is a catalyst for personal growth. By confronting our fears and uncertainties, we challenge ourselves to step outside our comfort zones. This process of exploration and self-discovery can lead to newfound strengths, skills, and resilience. For example, someone who openly discusses their struggles with mental health can gain insights into their coping mechanisms and develop healthier strategies for managing their emotions.
3. **Authenticity**: Living authentically requires embracing our vulnerabilities. When we accept and acknowledge our imperfections, we become more genuine in our interactions with others. Authenticity fosters self-acceptance and encourages others to embrace their true selves, creating a culture of openness and understanding.

4. **Empathy and Compassion**: Vulnerability cultivates empathy and compassion, both for ourselves and for others. When we share our struggles, we allow others to see our humanity, which can inspire them to share their experiences. This exchange creates a sense of belonging and mutual support, reinforcing the idea that we are not alone in our challenges.
5. **Courage and Resilience**: Embracing vulnerability requires courage. Each time we allow ourselves to be vulnerable, we build resilience and develop a stronger sense of self. This resilience enables us to navigate life's challenges with greater ease, as we learn to trust ourselves and our ability to cope with adversity.

Practical Steps to Embrace Vulnerability

1. **Acknowledge Your Feelings**: The first step in embracing vulnerability is acknowledging your feelings and recognizing when you feel vulnerable. Take time to reflect on situations that trigger feelings of fear, anxiety, or uncertainty. Journaling can be an effective way to process your emotions and gain clarity about your experiences.
2. **Share Your Story**: Begin by sharing your experiences with trusted friends or family members. Vulnerability is often easier in safe spaces where you feel supported. By sharing your story, you create an opportunity for others to connect with you on a deeper level.
3. **Practice Self-Compassion**: Treat yourself with kindness and understanding, especially during moments of vulnerability. Self-compassion allows you to recognize that everyone struggles and that it's okay to be imperfect. Speak to yourself as you would to a friend facing a similar challenge.
4. **Seek Support**: Surround yourself with supportive individuals who encourage vulnerability. Share your thoughts and feelings with those who value authenticity and openness. Joining support groups or communities can also provide a sense of belonging and understanding.
5. **Challenge Negative Beliefs**: Identify and challenge any negative beliefs you hold about vulnerability. Replace thoughts like "I'll be judged" or "I can't show weakness" with more empowering statements such as "I deserve to be heard" and "Vulnerability is a strength."
6. **Take Small Steps**: Start with small acts of vulnerability and gradually build your comfort level. This could involve sharing a personal story in a

group setting or expressing your feelings to a close friend. Each step you take will reinforce your belief in the strength of vulnerability.

Vulnerability in Practice

Real-life examples of individuals finding strength in vulnerability abound. Consider the stories of public figures who have openly discussed their struggles with mental health, addiction, or personal loss. Their willingness to share their experiences has not only helped them heal but has also provided comfort and inspiration to countless others facing similar challenges.

Moreover, in professional settings, leaders who embrace vulnerability foster a culture of openness and innovation. When leaders share their own struggles and failures, they create an environment where team members feel safe to take risks, voice their concerns, and propose new ideas. This culture of vulnerability leads to increased collaboration, creativity, and overall team success.

Finding strength in vulnerability is a transformative journey that can lead to deeper connections, personal growth, and enhanced authenticity. By challenging societal misconceptions and embracing vulnerability, we unlock our true potential and foster meaningful relationships with ourselves and others. Vulnerability is not a weakness; it is a testament to our courage and resilience. As we learn to navigate our vulnerabilities with grace and compassion, we create a more empathetic world where everyone feels seen, heard, and valued. Ultimately, embracing vulnerability can lead to a richer, more fulfilling life, where we can thrive despite the uncertainties we face.

EIGHT

Overcoming Fear and Failure

In the journey of personal growth, overcoming fear and failure is a pivotal chapter that empowers individuals to break free from self-imposed limitations and embrace their true potential. Fear often acts as a formidable barrier, preventing us from pursuing our dreams and taking risks. It can manifest in various forms—fear of the unknown, fear of rejection, or fear of inadequacy—each with the potential to paralyze our progress. Similarly, the experience of failure, while often viewed negatively, holds valuable lessons that can lead to profound personal development. In this chapter, we explore the nature of fear and failure, emphasizing the importance of reframing these experiences as opportunities for learning and growth. By cultivating resilience and adopting a growth mindset, we can transform our relationship with fear and failure, allowing us to take bold steps forward. Through personal anecdotes, research insights, and practical strategies, this chapter aims to inspire readers to face their fears head-on, embrace failure as a stepping stone to success, and ultimately unlock their potential for a more fulfilling and courageous life.

The Gift of Failure

Failure is often seen as a negative experience, something to be avoided at all costs. From a young age, many of us are conditioned to associate failure with disappointment, shame, and a sense of inadequacy. However, a growing body of research and lived experiences suggests that failure can be one of the most profound teachers we encounter on our journey through life. When we shift our perspective on failure, recognizing it as an opportunity for growth, we can begin to appreciate the invaluable lessons it offers. This essay explores the concept of failure, its benefits, and how embracing failure can lead to personal development and success.

Redefining Failure

To understand the gift of failure, we must first redefine what failure means to us. Traditionally, failure is viewed as falling short of our goals, making mistakes, or not meeting expectations. However, if we view failure as a natural part of the learning process, we can start to see it as an essential stepping stone toward growth and improvement. Failure provides critical feedback, highlighting areas where we can learn, adapt, and enhance our skills. This perspective encourages a mindset that values effort, perseverance, and resilience.

The Benefits of Failure

1. **Learning Opportunities**: One of the most significant gifts of failure is the opportunity to learn. When we fail, we are confronted with the reality of our limitations and mistakes. This confrontation compels us to analyze what went wrong and identify strategies for improvement. Each failure provides us with insights that can inform our future decisions and actions, ultimately guiding us toward success.
2. **Resilience Building**: Experiencing failure helps us build resilience—the ability to bounce back from setbacks. When we encounter challenges and disappointments, we learn to adapt and find alternative solutions. Resilience is not just about enduring hardship; it is about emerging from those experiences stronger and more determined. Each time we face failure and continue to persevere, we reinforce our capacity to withstand future challenges.
3. **Clarifying Goals**: Failure can also serve as a powerful tool for clarifying our goals and values. When we fall short of our expectations, it prompts us to reassess our ambitions and motivations. Are we pursuing goals that truly resonate with us, or are we influenced by external pressures? This reflection can lead to a more authentic path, guiding us toward endeavors that align with our passions and aspirations.
4. **Fostering Creativity**: The fear of failure can stifle creativity and innovation. When we allow ourselves to fail, we create space for experimentation and exploration. Failure encourages us to think outside the box, take risks, and pursue unconventional solutions. This creative mindset is crucial in fields such as art, science, and business, where innovation thrives on the willingness to take chances and learn from the

outcomes.

5. **Cultivating Empathy**: Experiencing failure can deepen our empathy for others. When we face our own struggles and setbacks, we become more compassionate and understanding toward the challenges others encounter. This empathy fosters stronger relationships and builds supportive communities where individuals can share their experiences without fear of judgment.

Embracing Failure in Practice

To fully appreciate the gift of failure, we must actively embrace it in our lives. Here are some practical strategies for cultivating a healthier relationship with failure:

1. **Change Your Narrative**: Begin by reframing your internal dialogue about failure. Instead of viewing it as a reflection of your worth or capabilities, see it as a valuable learning experience. Remind yourself that everyone fails at some point and that failure is an integral part of the journey toward success.
2. **Set Realistic Expectations**: While ambition is important, setting realistic and attainable goals can help mitigate the fear of failure. Break larger goals into smaller, manageable steps, allowing for incremental progress. This approach reduces the pressure to succeed immediately and creates space for learning and growth.
3. **Practice Self-Compassion**: Be kind to yourself when you encounter failure. Acknowledge your feelings of disappointment or frustration, but also recognize that these feelings are part of being human. Treat yourself with the same compassion you would extend to a friend facing a similar situation.
4. **Seek Feedback**: Constructive feedback is essential for growth. After experiencing failure, seek input from trusted friends, mentors, or colleagues. Their perspectives can provide valuable insights and help you identify areas for improvement. Embrace feedback as a tool for learning rather than as criticism.
5. **Celebrate Small Wins**: In the face of failure, it's crucial to acknowledge and celebrate small successes along the way. Recognizing your progress, no matter how minor, can boost your motivation and reinforce the idea that growth is a gradual process.

6. **Share Your Story**: Openly sharing your experiences with failure can help normalize the conversation around it. Whether through personal anecdotes, blogs, or public speaking, sharing your journey can inspire others to embrace their failures and view them as opportunities for growth.

Real-Life Examples of the Gift of Failure

Many renowned figures have experienced failure on their paths to success, illustrating the transformative power of embracing setbacks. For instance, Thomas Edison famously failed over a thousand times before successfully inventing the light bulb. Instead of viewing these failures as obstacles, Edison saw them as steppingstones, each one bringing him closer to his goal.

Similarly, J.K. Rowling faced numerous rejections before finding a publisher for the "Harry Potter" series. Her initial failures did not deter her; instead, they fueled her determination to share her story with the world. Today, she is one of the most successful authors in history, reminding us that perseverance in the face of failure can lead to extraordinary outcomes.

In the realm of business, many successful entrepreneurs have faced significant setbacks before achieving their goals. For instance, Howard Schultz, the former CEO of Starbucks, experienced rejection when trying to secure funding for his vision. Rather than giving up, he used the feedback to refine his approach and ultimately built a global coffee empire.

The gift of failure lies in its ability to teach, transform, and empower us. By shifting our perspective on failure, we can uncover valuable lessons that contribute to our personal and professional growth. Embracing failure allows us to cultivate resilience, clarify our goals, foster creativity, and deepen our empathy for others. As we learn to view failure as a natural and essential part of our journey, we unlock our true potential and open ourselves up to new opportunities. In a world that often prioritizes success over the process, it is crucial to celebrate the gift of failure and recognize its role in shaping who we are and who we aspire to become.

Building Courage and Confidence

Courage and confidence are essential qualities that empower individuals to navigate life's challenges, pursue their passions, and achieve personal growth. While they are often perceived as innate traits possessed by only a few, courage and confidence can actually be cultivated and developed over time. Building these qualities involves a conscious effort to confront fears, embrace vulnerability, and take action despite uncertainties. This essay explores the foundations of courage and confidence, the steps to develop them, and the profound impact they can have on our lives.

Understanding Courage and Confidence

Courage is the ability to confront fear, pain, or adversity despite feeling afraid. It does not mean the absence of fear; rather, it is the decision to act in spite of it. Courage can manifest in various forms, from speaking up in a challenging situation to taking risks in pursuit of a dream. Confidence, on the other hand, refers to the belief in one's abilities and judgment. It is the assurance that we can navigate obstacles and overcome challenges. Together, courage and confidence create a powerful synergy, enabling us to pursue our goals with determination and resilience.

The Importance of Courage and Confidence

1. **Overcoming Fear**: Fear is a natural human emotion that can paralyze us and prevent us from taking action. Building courage allows us to confront our fears head-on, whether they stem from public speaking, starting a new job, or pursuing a personal goal. By developing courage, we learn to see fear as a steppingstone rather than a barrier.
2. **Taking Risks**: Confidence encourages us to take calculated risks, which are often necessary for growth and success. When we believe in our abilities, we are more likely to step outside our comfort zones and seize opportunities that come our way. This willingness to take risks can lead to new experiences and achievements.
3. **Resilience in Adversity**: Life is full of challenges and setbacks. Courage and confidence enable us to face adversity with a positive mindset. Instead of succumbing to despair, individuals with these qualities are more likely to persevere and find solutions to their problems.
4. **Enhancing Relationships**: Building courage and confidence also improves our relationships with others. When we are confident in ourselves, we are more likely to express our thoughts and feelings honestly. This openness fosters deeper connections and allows for more meaningful interactions with others.

Steps to Build Courage and Confidence

1. **Acknowledge Your Fears**: The first step in building courage is recognizing and acknowledging your fears. Take time to reflect on what

holds you back. Identifying your fears allows you to confront them rather than avoid them. Write down your fears and analyze how they affect your decisions.

2. **Set Small Goals**: Building courage and confidence is a gradual process. Start by setting small, achievable goals that push you out of your comfort zone. For example, if public speaking terrifies you, start by sharing your ideas in smaller group settings before progressing to larger audiences. Each small success will bolster your confidence and encourage you to tackle bigger challenges.
3. **Practice Self-Compassion**: Being kind to yourself is crucial in the journey of building courage and confidence. Understand that everyone experiences setbacks and makes mistakes. Instead of criticizing yourself, practice self-compassion. Treat yourself with the same kindness you would offer a friend facing similar challenges.
4. **Seek Support**: Surround yourself with supportive individuals who encourage and uplift you. Sharing your aspirations and fears with trusted friends or mentors can provide valuable perspectives and motivation. Having a support system helps reinforce your courage and confidence as you navigate challenges.
5. **Embrace Vulnerability**: Courage often requires embracing vulnerability. Allow yourself to be open about your feelings and uncertainties. Vulnerability fosters authenticity and creates opportunities for deeper connections with others. When you acknowledge your vulnerabilities, you can also recognize your strengths, leading to greater confidence.
6. **Celebrate Progress**: Acknowledge and celebrate your achievements, no matter how small. Recognizing your progress reinforces your belief in your abilities and encourages you to continue pushing your boundaries. Keeping a journal to document your successes can serve as a powerful reminder of your growth over time.

Building courage and confidence is a transformative journey that empowers individuals to face their fears, take risks, and achieve their goals. By understanding the importance of these qualities and taking deliberate steps to cultivate them, we can unlock our full potential and navigate life's challenges with resilience and determination. Courage and confidence are not inherent traits but rather skills that can be developed through practice, self-reflection, and support. As we embark on this journey, we discover that embracing courage and confidence leads not only to personal growth but also to richer, more meaningful experiences in life.

Transforming Setbacks into Opportunities

Life is often a series of ups and downs, with setbacks and challenges serving as common experiences for everyone. While setbacks can be disheartening, they also hold the potential to be transformative moments that lead to personal growth, resilience, and new opportunities. The ability to turn setbacks into opportunities is a crucial skill that can significantly affect our lives, both personally and professionally. This essay explores the nature of setbacks, how to reframe them as opportunities, and the strategies for navigating these challenging times effectively.

Understanding Setbacks

Setbacks can take many forms, including failures in our careers, personal relationships, health challenges, or financial difficulties. These experiences often evoke feelings of disappointment, frustration, and hopelessness. The key to transforming these setbacks lies in our mindset—the way we perceive and respond to these challenges.

When faced with a setback, we can either succumb to negativity and defeat or adopt a more constructive attitude that allows us to learn and grow from the experience. This perspective shift is essential, as it can determine the outcome of our efforts to overcome obstacles and capitalize on new opportunities.

The Power of Reframing

Reframing is a powerful cognitive technique that involves changing our perspective on a situation. By viewing setbacks as temporary hurdles rather than permanent failures, we can cultivate a mindset that is open to learning and growth. Here are several ways to reframe setbacks:

1. **Learning Experiences**: Instead of seeing setbacks as failures, we can view them as valuable learning experiences. Each setback provides insights that can help us make better decisions in the future. For instance, a business venture that fails can teach an entrepreneur about market dynamics, customer preferences, and strategic planning.
2. **Opportunities for Growth**: Setbacks can serve as catalysts for personal growth. When we encounter challenges, we are often pushed to step outside our comfort zones and develop new skills or resilience. This growth can lead to greater self-awareness and confidence, enabling us to tackle future challenges more effectively.

3. **Redirection**: Sometimes, setbacks can redirect us toward paths that align more closely with our true goals and passions. A job loss, for example, can prompt an individual to reevaluate their career trajectory and explore opportunities that they may not have considered otherwise. This redirection can ultimately lead to more fulfilling and meaningful pursuits.
4. **Building Resilience**: Each setback we encounter can strengthen our resilience—the ability to bounce back from adversity. By facing and overcoming challenges, we develop coping mechanisms and strategies that make us more capable of handling future difficulties. This resilience is a valuable asset that can serve us throughout our lives.

Strategies for Transforming Setbacks into Opportunities

While reframing setbacks is an essential first step, there are practical strategies that can help us transform these challenges into opportunities:

1. **Accept and Acknowledge**: The first step in overcoming a setback is to accept and acknowledge the situation. Denial can prolong feelings of frustration and helplessness. Instead, face the reality of the setback head-on. Acceptance allows you to process your emotions and begin to move forward.
2. **Reflect and Analyze**: Take time to reflect on the setback. What went wrong? What could you have done differently? Analyzing the situation provides valuable insights that can inform your future decisions. This reflection can also help you identify patterns or behaviors that may have contributed to the setback.
3. **Set New Goals**: After reflecting on the setback, set new goals that align with your current circumstances. These goals should be realistic and achievable, providing you with a clear direction moving forward. Breaking these goals down into smaller, actionable steps can make the process feel more manageable and less overwhelming.
4. **Seek Support**: Don't hesitate to seek support from friends, family, or mentors. Sharing your experiences and feelings can provide valuable perspective and encouragement. Additionally, others may offer insights or resources that you hadn't considered, helping you navigate the situation more effectively.
5. **Maintain a Positive Mindset**: Cultivating a positive mindset can significantly influence how you respond to setbacks. Practice gratitude

by focusing on what you have learned from the experience and the strengths you possess. Surround yourself with positive influences and engage in activities that uplift your spirits.

6. **Take Action**: Once you have reflected, analyzed, and set new goals, take action. Procrastination can lead to feelings of stagnation and defeat. Taking small steps toward your goals can create momentum and build confidence. Each action you take reinforces the belief that you are capable of overcoming challenges.
7. **Embrace Flexibility**: Life is unpredictable, and setbacks often require us to be flexible in our approach. Embrace adaptability and be willing to pivot your plans as needed. This flexibility allows you to respond effectively to changing circumstances and seize new opportunities that arise.

Real-Life Examples of Transformation

Many individuals and organizations have successfully transformed setbacks into opportunities, illustrating the power of resilience and adaptability. For example, the well-known entrepreneur Richard Branson faced multiple setbacks in his career, including the failure of his airline, Virgin Atlantic, and several other ventures. Rather than being deterred, Branson viewed these failures as learning experiences, leading him to launch successful enterprises in different industries, including music, telecommunications, and space travel.

Similarly, J.K. Rowling experienced numerous rejections before finding a publisher for the "Harry Potter" series. Each rejection could have discouraged her, but instead, she persevered, using the feedback to refine her work. Ultimately, her determination led to one of the most successful book series in history, inspiring millions of readers around the world.

Transforming setbacks into opportunities is a vital skill that can significantly impact our personal and professional lives. By reframing setbacks as learning experiences and adopting a proactive mindset, we can unlock the potential for growth and resilience. The journey through setbacks is often challenging, but it can also be an avenue for self-discovery, empowerment, and new beginnings. As we learn to navigate life's challenges, we become more equipped to embrace opportunities and pursue our goals with confidence and determination. Embracing setbacks not only strengthens our character but also enriches our journey, reminding us that every challenge holds the potential for transformation.

NINE

In the journey of life, patience and persistence emerge as essential virtues that empower individuals to navigate challenges and achieve their long-term goals. This chapter delves into the profound impact that these qualities can have on personal growth and success. Patience allows us to endure setbacks, maintaining a sense of calm and clarity as we await the fruition of our efforts. It teaches us that great things often take time, urging us to resist the temptation of instant gratification. On the other hand, persistence drives us to keep pushing forward despite obstacles and discouragement. It is the unwavering commitment to our goals, reminding us that failure is not the end but a steppingstone toward eventual success. Together, patience and persistence create a powerful synergy that enables us to overcome adversity, adapt to changing circumstances, and remain focused on our aspirations. By cultivating these virtues, we learn that the journey itself is as important as the destination, fostering resilience and a deeper appreciation for the process of growth and achievement.

Learning the Value of Waiting

In a world that often champions immediacy and instant gratification, the value of waiting can seem like an outdated concept. However, the ability to wait—whether for personal goals, opportunities, or relationships—can yield profound benefits. Learning to appreciate and embrace the process of waiting fosters resilience, patience, and ultimately, a deeper understanding of ourselves and the world around us. This essay explores the significance of waiting, the lessons it teaches, and how embracing this virtue can lead to personal growth.

The Nature of Waiting

Waiting is an inherent part of life. From the simple act of waiting in line to more complex scenarios such as awaiting job offers, healing from a setback, or anticipating significant life changes, waiting is unavoidable. While it can often be frustrating, especially in a fast-paced society, waiting serves as an opportunity for reflection and growth. It invites us to step back, reassess our priorities, and cultivate a sense of patience that can enhance our overall well-being.

Cultivating Patience

One of the most significant lessons learned through waiting is the cultivation of patience. Patience is not merely the act of sitting idle but is an active process that involves maintaining a calm and composed mindset during periods of uncertainty. It allows us to develop a deeper understanding of ourselves and our desires. By practicing patience, we can learn to control impulsive behaviors and make thoughtful decisions rather than succumbing to hasty choices.

For example, when pursuing long-term goals, such as completing an education or building a career, the journey can often be slow and filled with challenges. Instead of feeling disheartened by delays, embracing patience can empower us to appreciate the incremental progress we make. This mindset can lead to greater satisfaction and fulfillment when we eventually achieve our goals.

Reflection and Growth

Waiting also provides a valuable opportunity for reflection. During periods of waiting, we can take time to evaluate our motivations, desires, and the choices we've made thus far. This introspection can reveal insights that may have been overlooked during busier times. By examining our feelings and experiences, we gain clarity about what truly matters to us, allowing us to align our actions with our values.

Furthermore, the process of waiting encourages personal growth. Challenges faced during waiting periods—such as doubt, anxiety, or frustration—can teach us essential coping skills and resilience. By confronting and navigating these emotions, we emerge stronger and more equipped to handle future challenges.

Building Resilience

Resilience is another crucial lesson learned from waiting. Life rarely unfolds according to our timelines, and setbacks can often test our determination and resolve. Waiting teaches us to embrace uncertainty and adapt to changing circumstances. It fosters a mindset that recognizes that perseverance is essential to success.

For instance, consider an athlete training for a competition. The journey is filled with rigorous training sessions, injuries, and periods of doubt. However, those who learn to wait, persist, and trust the process are often the ones who succeed in achieving their goals. This resilience, built through the practice of waiting, becomes a valuable asset that extends beyond the athletic realm into all areas of life.

Embracing the Journey

Ultimately, learning the value of waiting invites us to embrace the journey rather than fixate solely on the destination. In a culture that often prioritizes speed and efficiency, recognizing the beauty in the process can be transformative. The moments spent waiting can become opportunities for connection, learning, and self-discovery.

Whether waiting for a promotion, the resolution of a personal challenge, or the growth of a relationship, embracing the waiting period can lead to richer experiences. It allows us to build anticipation and excitement for what lies ahead, reinforcing the idea that the journey is as meaningful as the outcome.

learning the value of waiting is an essential skill that enhances our personal growth and resilience. It teaches us patience, encourages reflection, builds resilience, and allows us to embrace the journey of life fully. By cultivating an appreciation for waiting, we can navigate challenges with grace and confidence, ultimately enriching our experiences and fostering a deeper understanding of ourselves and the world around us. Rather than viewing waiting as a burden, we can learn to see it as an opportunity—a chance to grow, reflect, and prepare for the future.

The Role of Hard Work and Consistency

In the pursuit of success, two fundamental principles stand out: hard work and consistency. While talent and opportunity may play crucial roles, it is often the combination of relentless effort and unwavering dedication that ultimately leads to achievement. Hard work encompasses the physical and mental energy invested in a task, while consistency refers to the ability to maintain that effort over time. Together, they create a powerful synergy that can propel individuals toward their goals, regardless of the challenges they may face.

The Essence of Hard Work

Hard work is the cornerstone of success in any endeavor. It embodies the willingness to put in the time and effort required to hone skills, learn new concepts, and overcome obstacles. The value of hard work extends beyond mere physical labor; it also involves mental fortitude and resilience. When individuals commit to working hard, they cultivate a growth mindset—a belief that their abilities can be developed through dedication and effort.

For example, consider an aspiring musician. The road to mastery is often paved with countless hours of practice, failures, and learning experiences. Musicians who put in the hard work to practice consistently will likely outperform those who rely solely on innate talent. This principle applies across various fields, whether in athletics, academics, or business. Hard work builds a strong foundation for success and fosters discipline, perseverance, and confidence.

The Power of Consistency

While hard work lays the groundwork for achievement, consistency is what sustains progress over time. It is not enough to work hard sporadically; individuals must be committed to maintaining that effort regularly. Consistency allows individuals to create habits that drive them toward their goals, transforming their efforts into tangible results.

A great example of this is seen in the realm of fitness. Individuals who engage in regular exercise, regardless of the intensity, are more likely to achieve their health goals than those who engage in extreme workouts infrequently. Consistent effort, even when small, compounds over time, leading to significant improvements in performance and well-being. This principle holds true in various contexts, including studying for exams, developing a craft, or pursuing a professional career.

The Synergy of Hard Work and Consistency

The real magic happens when hard work and consistency come together. This synergy creates a powerful momentum that can lead to extraordinary outcomes. When individuals are both dedicated and consistent in their efforts, they develop a sense of accountability and responsibility toward their goals.

For instance, successful entrepreneurs often embody this synergy. They put in the hard work to develop their ideas, but they also maintain consistency in their efforts to innovate, adapt, and improve their businesses. This continuous dedication helps them navigate the inevitable challenges and setbacks they encounter. By consistently evaluating their strategies and adjusting their approaches, they remain resilient and better positioned to seize opportunities.

Learning from Setbacks

Hard work and consistency also play vital roles in how individuals respond to setbacks. Life is filled with obstacles and failures, but those who embrace hard work and consistency are often better equipped to handle adversity. When challenges arise, their established habits and commitment to their goals help them remain focused and motivated.

For example, a student facing academic challenges may feel discouraged after receiving a poor grade. However, if they have consistently put in the effort to study and learn, they are more likely to seek help, revise their strategies, and ultimately improve. This proactive approach, rooted in hard work and consistency, enables them to turn setbacks into learning experiences and propel themselves forward.

In conclusion, hard work and consistency are indispensable elements in the pursuit of success. While talent and opportunity are important, they are often eclipsed by the determination and commitment demonstrated through hard work and the sustained effort shown through consistency. Together, these qualities create a powerful framework for achieving goals, overcoming challenges, and ultimately realizing one's full potential. Embracing hard work and consistency not only leads to tangible results but also fosters personal growth, resilience, and a deep sense of accomplishment. As individuals learn to navigate their journeys with these principles in mind, they cultivate a mindset that empowers them to chase their dreams relentlessly and achieve success in their endeavors.

Balancing Effort and Surrender

In a world that often celebrates hustle, ambition, and relentless pursuit, the concept of surrender can seem counterintuitive. However, balancing effort and surrender is essential for achieving holistic well-being and long-term success. While effort is crucial for driving progress and accomplishing goals, surrender allows us to release the need for control and accept life's uncertainties. This balance creates a harmonious approach to life, enabling individuals to navigate challenges with grace, resilience, and a deeper sense of fulfillment.

The Nature of Effort

Effort is the driving force behind achievement. It represents the physical, emotional, and mental energy we invest in our pursuits. Whether it's striving for career advancement, cultivating relationships, or enhancing personal skills, effort is the catalyst that propels us forward. It embodies determination, discipline, and hard work.

In various fields, effort manifests differently. For example, athletes commit countless hours to training, refining their techniques, and pushing their limits to excel in their sports. Similarly, students engage in rigorous study routines to master subjects and achieve academic excellence. This dedicated effort is crucial for developing skills, acquiring knowledge, and reaching goals.

However, while effort is necessary, it can also lead to burnout if not managed effectively. The constant drive to achieve can create pressure and stress, leading to physical and mental exhaustion. This is where the concept of surrender becomes vital.

Understanding Surrender

Surrender often carries negative connotations, suggesting defeat or giving up. However, in a more nuanced sense, surrender is about acceptance and letting go of the need to control every outcome. It involves trusting the process and recognizing that some factors are beyond our influence. Surrender allows us to release our attachments to specific outcomes and embrace the uncertainty of life.

In the context of personal growth, surrender is a powerful tool for fostering resilience and adaptability. When we surrender, we create space for new possibilities, perspectives, and experiences. Instead of rigidly adhering to a predefined plan, surrender invites us to flow with life's changes and challenges. This mindset promotes mental well-being and emotional balance, enabling us to respond to adversity with grace.

The Dance Between Effort and Surrender

The challenge lies in finding the right balance between effort and surrender. Both are essential components of a fulfilling life, but they can easily become out of sync. Striking this balance involves understanding when to exert effort and when to surrender to the flow of life.

1. **Recognizing Limits**: One of the first steps in balancing effort and surrender is recognizing our limits. While it's important to strive for excellence, it's equally vital to acknowledge when we've reached our capacity. Overcommitting and pushing ourselves beyond our limits can lead to burnout and frustration. By understanding our boundaries, we can apply effort more strategically, allowing for periods of rest and rejuvenation.
2. **Cultivating Mindfulness**: Mindfulness plays a crucial role in maintaining the balance between effort and surrender. By staying

present and aware of our thoughts and feelings, we can better assess our needs and reactions. Mindfulness allows us to discern when to push ourselves and when to step back. Through practices like meditation and reflective journaling, we can cultivate a deeper understanding of our inner selves, leading to more informed decisions.

3. **Embracing Flexibility**: Life is inherently unpredictable, and plans often change. Embracing flexibility is essential for balancing effort and surrender. While setting goals and working toward them is important, being open to adapting our strategies and expectations can lead to greater satisfaction. This flexibility allows us to respond effectively to unexpected challenges and seize new opportunities.
4. **Trusting the Process**: Trusting the process is a vital aspect of surrender. It requires faith in our journey, even when outcomes are uncertain. This trust allows us to release our attachment to specific results and focus on the present moment. By trusting the process, we can appreciate the lessons and experiences gained along the way, regardless of the final outcome.

Real-Life Examples of Balance

Many individuals have successfully navigated the balance between effort and surrender, illustrating the transformative power of this dynamic relationship. For instance, consider the journey of an entrepreneur. Building a business requires immense effort—long hours, strategic planning, and unwavering determination. However, successful entrepreneurs also recognize the importance of surrendering to market forces, customer feedback, and unexpected challenges. By balancing their efforts with a willingness to adapt and learn, they can create resilient and thriving enterprises.

Similarly, in the realm of personal relationships, balancing effort and surrender can enhance connection and intimacy. Individuals may invest significant effort into nurturing their relationships through communication, support, and shared experiences. Yet, they must also surrender the need to control every aspect of the relationship, allowing space for vulnerability and authenticity. This balance fosters deeper connections and a more profound understanding of one another.

The Role of Self-Compassion

Self-compassion is a crucial component of balancing effort and surrender. When we approach our pursuits with self-compassion, we cultivate a mindset that embraces imperfections and setbacks. Instead of criticizing ourselves for perceived failures, we learn to treat ourselves with kindness and understanding. This self-compassion allows us to navigate challenges with greater resilience, making it easier to surrender to life's uncertainties.

Moreover, self-compassion fosters a sense of balance between effort and surrender. It encourages us to recognize our hard work while also granting permission to take breaks and seek help when needed. By practicing self-compassion, we can create a healthier relationship with our goals and aspirations.

Balancing effort and surrender is essential for navigating the complexities of life with grace and resilience. While effort drives progress and achievement, surrender allows us to embrace uncertainty and trust the process. Striking this balance requires self-awareness, mindfulness, and flexibility, enabling us to respond effectively to life's challenges.

Ultimately, learning to balance effort and surrender can lead to a more fulfilling and meaningful existence. It encourages us to pursue our goals with dedication while also appreciating the journey, learning from setbacks, and embracing the beauty of uncertainty. In a world that often prioritizes constant striving, finding harmony between these two principles can unlock new levels of personal growth, well-being, and authentic living.

TEN

Part IV: Lessons on Purpose and Fulfillment

Part IV of this exploration delves into the profound lessons on purpose and fulfillment that guide us through life's journey. Understanding one's purpose is essential for navigating the complexities of existence, as it provides a clear direction and meaning to our actions. This section emphasizes the importance of discovering what truly resonates within us, aligning our goals with our core values, and cultivating a sense of fulfillment that transcends mere accomplishments. Through personal anecdotes, philosophical insights, and practical strategies, readers are encouraged to reflect on their unique paths, recognize the significance of their contributions, and embrace a life rich in intention. By uncovering the interplay between purpose and fulfillment, we learn that true contentment arises not from external validation but from the deep connection we forge with our passions, relationships, and the world around us. This journey of self-discovery empowers us to live authentically, fostering a sense of belonging and significance that enriches our lives and the lives of those we touch.

Chapter 10: Finding Meaning in Life

Discovering Your Life's Purpose

Finding one's life purpose is a quest that many embark on at various stages of their lives. It is an intricate journey filled with self-discovery, introspection, and exploration. A sense of purpose provides direction, motivation, and fulfillment, transforming mundane existence into a life imbued with meaning. While the search for purpose can be daunting, it is also one of the most rewarding endeavors one can undertake. This exploration encourages individuals to connect with their inner selves, understand their values, and identify what truly matters to them.

The Importance of Purpose

The significance of having a purpose in life cannot be overstated. Research has shown that individuals with a strong sense of purpose experience greater life satisfaction, better mental health, and improved physical well-being. Purpose acts as a compass, guiding decisions and helping people navigate challenges. When individuals understand their purpose, they are more likely to set meaningful goals, engage in activities that resonate with them, and foster resilience in the face of adversity.

Moreover, a well-defined purpose fosters a sense of belonging and community. It connects individuals to something larger than themselves, whether it be through contributing to society, nurturing relationships, or pursuing passions. This sense of connection enhances overall well-being and encourages individuals to take proactive steps towards creating a positive impact in the world.

Reflecting on Personal Values

The journey to discovering one's purpose begins with introspection and self-reflection. Understanding personal values is a fundamental step in this process. Values are the guiding principles that shape our decisions, behaviors, and interactions with the world. They reflect what is most important to us and serve as a foundation for our beliefs and actions.

To identify personal values, individuals can engage in various reflective exercises. Journaling can be a helpful tool, allowing for the exploration of thoughts and feelings. Questions such as, "What brings me joy?" "What do I stand for?" and "What activities make me lose track of time?" can provide insight into core values. Additionally, contemplating significant life experiences and the lessons learned from them can reveal underlying values that inform one's purpose.

Embracing Passions and Interests

Another key aspect of discovering life's purpose is recognizing passions and interests. What activities excite and energize us? What topics do we find ourselves drawn to? By exploring these passions, individuals can gain valuable insights into what makes their lives meaningful.

Engaging in diverse activities—whether through volunteering, pursuing hobbies, or taking courses—can help uncover hidden passions. For example, someone who enjoys painting may discover a purpose in using art as a means of expression and healing for others. Alternatively, a love for nature may lead to a commitment to environmental conservation. The key is to remain open to experiences and allow curiosity to guide exploration.

Setting Meaningful Goals

Once individuals have reflected on their values and passions, the next step is to set meaningful goals that align with their purpose. Goals provide a roadmap for achieving a sense of purpose and serve as motivators for personal growth. It is essential to set goals that resonate with one's values and passions, as this alignment fosters a sense of fulfillment.

When setting goals, it can be helpful to follow the SMART criteria—Specific, Measurable, Achievable, Relevant, and Time-bound. This framework ensures that goals are clear and attainable, allowing individuals to track their progress effectively. For example, if one's purpose involves helping others, a specific goal could be to volunteer at a local shelter for two hours each week. By breaking down larger aspirations into actionable steps, individuals can create a sense of momentum and accomplishment.

Overcoming Obstacles

The journey of discovering one's purpose is not without its challenges. Individuals may encounter obstacles such as self-doubt, fear of failure, or societal pressures that steer them away from their true calling. It is essential to acknowledge these feelings and understand that they are a natural part of the process.

To overcome self-doubt, individuals can practice self-compassion. Instead of being overly critical, they should treat themselves with kindness and recognize that growth takes time. Seeking support from friends, family, or mentors can also provide encouragement and perspective during difficult times. Sharing fears and aspirations with trusted individuals can lead to valuable insights and reaffirmation of one's journey.

Moreover, embracing a growth mindset—an understanding that abilities and intelligence can be developed through effort—can transform obstacles into opportunities for learning and growth. When individuals view setbacks as lessons rather than failures, they are more likely to persist in their pursuit of purpose.

The Role of Community

Finding purpose is often enhanced through connection with others. Engaging with like-minded individuals or communities can provide support, inspiration, and motivation. Collaborating with others who share similar values and passions fosters a sense of belonging and accountability.

Joining groups or organizations focused on shared interests—such as environmental activism, artistic endeavors, or community service—can create opportunities for connection and collaboration. These interactions not only enrich one's journey but also contribute to a greater sense of purpose by enabling individuals to work collectively toward a common goal.

Continuous Exploration and Growth

Discovering one's life purpose is not a destination but a continuous journey. As individuals grow and evolve, their values, passions, and aspirations may shift. It is essential to remain open to change and embrace new experiences. Regularly reflecting on one's journey allows for reassessment of goals and purpose.

Engaging in ongoing self-reflection, seeking new challenges, and being open to feedback can facilitate growth and deeper understanding. It is through this ongoing exploration that individuals can continue to align their lives with their evolving sense of purpose.

The journey of discovering one's life purpose is both profound and transformative. It requires introspection, exploration, and a willingness to embrace change. By reflecting on personal values, engaging with passions, setting meaningful goals, overcoming obstacles, and fostering community connections, individuals can uncover the essence of what makes their lives fulfilling.

Ultimately, understanding one's purpose enriches life experiences and fosters resilience, motivation, and satisfaction. This quest is a lifelong endeavor that leads to a deeper connection with oneself and the world, allowing individuals to live authentically and make meaningful contributions to their communities. Embracing this journey with an open heart and mind can lead to a life filled with purpose, passion, and fulfillment

Aligning Your Actions with Your Values

Aligning your actions with your values is a fundamental principle for leading a fulfilling and authentic life. When your behaviors and decisions are in harmony with your core beliefs, you experience greater satisfaction, purpose, and inner peace. Conversely, when there's a disconnect between what you believe and how you act, it can lead to feelings of confusion, frustration, and discontent. Understanding the importance of this alignment and taking proactive steps to achieve it can profoundly enhance your overall well-being.

Understanding Your Values

The first step in aligning actions with values is to clearly identify what those values are. Values serve as guiding principles that shape our thoughts, decisions, and behaviors. They can encompass a wide range of areas, including integrity, family, creativity, health, adventure, and community. To uncover your values, consider reflecting on significant moments in your life.

Ask yourself questions such as:

- What experiences have brought me the most joy?
- When have I felt most proud of myself?
- What issues am I passionate about?
- What qualities do I admire in others?

These reflections can help clarify your values, providing a foundation for making choices that resonate with your true self.

Evaluating Your Current Actions

Once you have a clearer understanding of your values, it's crucial to evaluate your current actions and behaviors. Take a close look at your daily activities, choices, and routines. Ask yourself whether they reflect your values or if they are influenced by external pressures, societal expectations, or fears.

For example, if one of your core values is family but you find yourself consistently prioritizing work over spending time with loved ones, this misalignment can lead to feelings of guilt and regret. Acknowledging these discrepancies is an essential step toward creating change.

Making Conscious Choices

Aligning your actions with your values requires conscious decision-making. Start by setting specific, actionable goals that reflect your values. If health is a priority, consider establishing a fitness routine or cooking healthier meals. If creativity matters to you, allocate time each week for artistic pursuits or hobbies.

It's also helpful to practice mindfulness, which allows you to stay present and aware of your choices. When faced with decisions, take a moment to pause and assess whether your options align with your values. This practice can empower you to make choices that resonate deeply within you.

Creating Boundaries

Establishing boundaries is another crucial aspect of aligning your actions with your values. It's important to protect your time and energy by saying no to commitments that do not support your core beliefs. For instance, if community service is one of your values, be selective about the projects you take on, ensuring they align with your passion for giving back.

Communicating your boundaries to others is essential for maintaining this alignment. Let friends, family, and colleagues know what is important to you, and be assertive in protecting your values. This may require difficult conversations, but it ultimately leads to healthier relationships and a more authentic life.

Embracing Flexibility

While it's essential to align your actions with your values, it's also important to remain flexible. Life is unpredictable, and circumstances may change, requiring adjustments to your plans and priorities. Embracing flexibility allows you to adapt without compromising your core values.

For example, if family is a core value but work demands increase unexpectedly, finding a balance that still allows for quality time with loved ones is key. This might mean adjusting your schedule or delegating tasks. The goal is not to rigidly adhere to a set routine but to ensure that your actions reflect your values, even in changing circumstances.

Regular Reflection and Reassessment

Aligning actions with values is an ongoing process that requires regular reflection and reassessment. Periodically take time to evaluate whether your actions continue to align with your core beliefs. This can involve journaling, meditation, or discussions with trusted friends or mentors.

As you grow and evolve, your values may shift, and that's perfectly normal. Being open to this evolution allows you to adapt your actions accordingly, ensuring that you remain true to yourself throughout life's journey.

Aligning your actions with your values is a transformative practice that leads to a more authentic, fulfilling, and purposeful life. By understanding your core beliefs, evaluating your current actions, making conscious choices, creating boundaries, embracing flexibility, and engaging in regular reflection, you can cultivate a lifestyle that resonates deeply with your true self. This alignment not only enhances your well-being but also empowers you to make a positive impact on the world around you, as you live authentically and contribute meaningfully to your community.

The Role of Passion in Fulfillment

Passion plays a critical role in the pursuit of fulfillment, serving as a driving force that fuels personal growth, motivates action, and cultivates a deeper sense of purpose. It is the intense enthusiasm or love for an activity, cause, or area of interest that invigorates our lives and helps us navigate challenges. When we engage with our passions, we not only enhance our individual experiences but also foster connections with others and contribute positively to our communities. Understanding the profound impact of passion on fulfillment can transform how we approach our personal and professional lives.

Defining Passion

Passion can be defined in various ways. At its core, it is a strong inclination towards something that we find enjoyable, meaningful, and rewarding. This could be an activity, such as painting, writing, cooking, or playing a sport, or it might be tied to a cause, such as environmental activism, social justice, or community service. When we pursue our passions, we often experience heightened feelings of happiness, excitement, and satisfaction, which are essential ingredients for a fulfilling life.

It's important to note that passion is not always linked to career choices. While some people may find their passion in their profession, others might pursue it as a hobby or volunteer opportunity. Regardless of the context, engaging with our passions allows us to express our true selves, explore our capabilities, and contribute to something greater than ourselves.

Passion as a Motivator

One of the most significant roles of passion in fulfillment is its capacity to serve as a powerful motivator. When we are passionate about something, we are more likely to dedicate our time and energy to it. This intrinsic motivation often translates into perseverance, enabling us to overcome obstacles and push through challenges that may arise along the way.

For instance, consider a musician who passionately loves creating and performing music. Despite facing numerous setbacks, such as rejection from record labels or difficult performances, their passion drives them to continue honing their craft. This unwavering dedication not only helps them improve their skills but also fosters resilience and the ability to bounce back from failure. As a result, their journey becomes not just about achieving success but about enjoying the process of growth and self-expression.

Enhancing Well-Being

Engaging in activities that ignite our passion contributes significantly to our overall well-being. Research has shown that pursuing one's passions is linked to higher levels of happiness, lower stress levels, and improved mental health. When we immerse ourselves in activities we love, we enter a state of flow—where time seems to stand still, and we lose ourselves in the moment. This state of flow promotes mindfulness and presence, allowing us to experience life more fully and deeply.

Moreover, passion can act as a buffer against life's challenges. During difficult times, having a passion to turn to can provide solace and distraction, helping individuals cope with stress and anxiety. For example, someone going through a tough period may find comfort in painting or gardening, using these activities as outlets for their emotions. The joy derived from engaging with their passion can serve as a vital source of strength, enabling them to navigate adversity with greater ease.

Fostering Connections

Another crucial aspect of passion is its ability to foster connections with others. When we engage with our passions, we often find ourselves in communities of like-minded individuals who share similar interests. These connections can lead to meaningful relationships, support systems, and collaborative opportunities, all of which enhance our sense of fulfillment.

For instance, joining a local hiking group can connect individuals with fellow nature enthusiasts, creating friendships rooted in shared experiences. These social interactions not only enrich our lives but also provide a sense of belonging and community, both of which are essential for our overall well-being. Moreover, sharing our passions with others can inspire them to pursue their interests, creating a ripple effect of enthusiasm and engagement that benefits everyone involved.

Passion and Purpose

The interplay between passion and purpose is a powerful one. While passion can ignite our interests, purpose gives those interests direction and meaning. When we align our passions with a greater purpose—such as contributing to social change or promoting environmental sustainability—we experience a deeper sense of fulfillment.

For example, someone passionate about cooking may find their purpose in using their culinary skills to provide meals for the homeless or teach cooking classes to underprivileged youth. This alignment not only enhances their sense of fulfillment but also allows them to make a positive impact in the lives of others. The combination of passion and purpose creates a powerful force that drives individuals to pursue their interests in ways that benefit both themselves and their communities.

Overcoming Challenges

While pursuing passions can be immensely rewarding, it can also come with challenges. Individuals may face societal expectations, financial constraints, or self-doubt that deter them from fully engaging with their interests. Overcoming these obstacles is essential for harnessing the transformative power of passion.

Developing a growth mindset—believing that abilities and intelligence can be cultivated through effort—can help individuals view challenges as opportunities for growth rather than insurmountable barriers. For example, an aspiring writer who struggles with self-doubt may benefit from seeking feedback, joining writing groups, or setting small, achievable goals to build confidence. By addressing challenges head-on, individuals can create a pathway toward fulfillment that is informed by their passions.

The role of passion in fulfillment is profound and multifaceted. By understanding and embracing our passions, we can enhance our motivation, well-being, and connections with others. Passion serves as a catalyst for personal growth, allowing us to navigate challenges and foster a sense of purpose in our lives. Whether it manifests in our careers, hobbies, or community engagements, passion is essential for creating a fulfilling and meaningful existence. As we embark on our unique journeys, let us not only pursue our passions but also share them with others, cultivating a world where enthusiasm and fulfillment thrive.

ELEVEN

In the journey toward fulfillment, gratitude and contentment emerge as powerful companions that can transform our perspectives and enhance our overall well-being. Gratitude involves recognizing and appreciating the positive aspects of our lives, whether they are big milestones or simple daily joys. It shifts our focus from what we lack to what we have, fostering a mindset that embraces abundance rather than scarcity. Contentment, on the other hand, is the inner peace that arises when we accept our circumstances, letting go of the constant pursuit of more. Together, gratitude and contentment cultivate a profound sense of happiness and satisfaction. This chapter explores how practicing gratitude can enrich our relationships, improve our mental health, and deepen our appreciation for life's experiences. By intentionally cultivating these qualities, we learn to find joy in the present moment and develop a resilient outlook that nurtures our emotional and psychological well-being. Ultimately, gratitude and contentment invite us to celebrate our journey, empowering us to navigate life's ups and downs with grace and positivity.

Practicing Daily Gratitude

Gratitude is more than just a fleeting feeling; it's a transformative practice that can significantly enhance our overall well-being and life satisfaction. When we consciously cultivate gratitude, we shift our focus from what we lack to what we have, fostering a deeper appreciation for the simple joys and blessings in our daily lives. Practicing daily gratitude can lead to profound changes in our perspectives, relationships, and even physical health. This exploration will delve into the benefits of gratitude, various methods to integrate it into our daily routines, and the positive ripple effects it can create.

Understanding the Benefits of Gratitude

Research has consistently shown that practicing gratitude can have a positive impact on mental and physical health. When we express gratitude, our brains release chemicals like dopamine and serotonin, which are associated with feelings of happiness and well-being. This biochemical response can create a positive feedback loop, encouraging us to engage in more gratitude-inducing activities.

Some of the notable benefits of gratitude include:

1. **Enhanced Mental Health**: Regularly practicing gratitude can lead to reduced symptoms of depression and anxiety. By focusing on positive experiences, we can counteract negative thoughts and feelings, improving our overall mood and outlook on life.
2. **Improved Relationships**: Expressing gratitude can strengthen relationships. Whether it's a heartfelt thank-you to a friend or acknowledging the support of a family member, expressing appreciation fosters deeper connections and mutual respect.
3. **Better Physical Health**: Grateful individuals often report fewer health complaints, more energy, and improved sleep quality. This could be linked to reduced stress levels and a more positive mindset, both of which contribute to better overall health.
4. **Increased Resilience**: Practicing gratitude can enhance our ability to cope with adversity. When faced with challenges, individuals who regularly express gratitude are more likely to maintain a positive outlook, find solutions, and bounce back from setbacks.

Incorporating Gratitude into Daily Life

Integrating gratitude into our daily routines doesn't have to be a daunting task. Here are some practical and effective methods for practicing daily gratitude:

1. **Gratitude Journaling**: One of the simplest yet most powerful ways to cultivate gratitude is through journaling. Set aside a few minutes each day to write down three to five things you are grateful for. These can be small, everyday occurrences, such as a warm cup of coffee, a kind gesture from a stranger, or a beautiful sunset. Over time, this practice can shift your focus toward the positive aspects of your life.
2. **Mindful Appreciation**: Take a moment each day to pause and mindfully appreciate your surroundings. This could involve noticing the beauty of nature, the comfort of your home, or the laughter of loved ones. Engaging your senses—sight, sound, smell, taste, and touch—can deepen your

appreciation for the present moment.

3. **Gratitude Letters**: Consider writing letters of gratitude to people who have positively impacted your life. Expressing your appreciation not only uplifts the recipient but also reinforces your own feelings of gratitude. Even if you don't send the letter, the act of writing it can be incredibly meaningful.
4. **Daily Affirmations**: Start or end your day with positive affirmations centered around gratitude. For example, you might say, "I am grateful for the opportunities this day brings" or "I appreciate the love and support in my life." These affirmations can set a positive tone for your day and reinforce a mindset of appreciation.
5. **Gratitude Rituals**: Create rituals that promote gratitude within your household or community. This could be a family dinner where everyone shares something they are grateful for, or a group gathering where participants express appreciation for one another. Such rituals can foster a sense of connection and collective positivity.
6. **Technology and Apps**: In our digital age, various apps can help facilitate daily gratitude practices. Consider using a gratitude app that prompts you to reflect on what you're thankful for each day. These apps often include reminders, inspiring quotes, and community features that can enhance your gratitude journey.

The Ripple Effects of Gratitude

Practicing daily gratitude not only benefits the individual but also creates a ripple effect that can positively influence those around us. When we express gratitude, we inspire others to do the same. For instance, a simple "thank you" can brighten someone's day and motivate them to spread kindness further. This cycle of appreciation can create a more compassionate and supportive environment in families, workplaces, and communities.

Moreover, gratitude fosters a culture of recognition and respect. In professional settings, expressing appreciation for colleagues' contributions can lead to a more engaged and motivated workforce. Teams that celebrate each other's successes are more likely to collaborate effectively and create a positive work atmosphere.

Overcoming Challenges to Gratitude

While practicing gratitude can be incredibly beneficial, it can also be challenging, especially during difficult times. Life's challenges, such as loss, stress, or uncertainty, can make it hard to focus on the positives. During these times, it's essential to acknowledge and honor our feelings while gently redirecting our focus toward gratitude.

One approach is to find gratitude in adversity. This doesn't mean minimizing pain or struggles but rather seeking lessons or silver linings amid challenges. For example, someone who loses a job may feel devastated initially but later recognizes the opportunity to pursue a more fulfilling career path. This shift in perspective can promote resilience and growth.

Practicing daily gratitude is a simple yet powerful tool for enhancing our well-being and enriching our lives. By incorporating gratitude into our daily routines, we can shift our focus from what we lack to what we have, fostering a greater sense of fulfillment, happiness, and connection. The benefits of gratitude extend beyond the individual, creating positive ripple effects in our relationships and communities. As we embrace gratitude, we cultivate a more optimistic outlook on life, enabling us to navigate challenges with resilience and appreciate the beauty of our everyday experiences. Whether through journaling, mindful appreciation, or expressing thanks to others, the practice of gratitude invites us to celebrate life in all its complexity and richness.

The Joy of Simple Living

In a world that often glorifies complexity and excess, the concept of simple living emerges as a refreshing and fulfilling alternative. Simple living is not merely a lifestyle choice; it is a philosophy that emphasizes the importance of minimalism, mindfulness, and intentionality in our daily lives. By embracing simplicity, we can cultivate joy, reduce stress, and create space for what truly matters. This exploration will delve into the principles of simple living, its myriad benefits, and practical steps to incorporate simplicity into our lives.

Understanding Simple Living

At its core, simple living revolves around the idea of simplifying our lives to focus on what is essential. This can manifest in various ways, such as decluttering physical possessions, reducing commitments, and prioritizing experiences over material possessions. Simple living encourages us to evaluate our values and priorities, enabling us to make choices that align with our authentic selves.

While simple living may look different for everyone, common themes include minimalism, sustainability, and mindfulness. Minimalism, for instance, is about removing the excess—be it material possessions, distractions, or commitments—that weighs us down. Sustainability emphasizes making choices that are environmentally responsible, promoting a healthier planet for future generations. Mindfulness involves being present in the moment and fully engaging with our experiences, fostering a deeper appreciation for life.

The Benefits of Simple Living

Embracing simple living can yield numerous benefits that enhance our overall well-being:

1. **Reduced Stress**: One of the most immediate benefits of simple living is a significant reduction in stress levels. By decluttering our environments and simplifying our schedules, we create a more peaceful and serene atmosphere. This simplicity allows us to focus on what truly matters, reducing the mental noise that often accompanies a hectic lifestyle.
2. **Increased Happiness**: The joy of simple living lies in its ability to cultivate genuine happiness. When we let go of the pursuit of material possessions and societal expectations, we can find joy in the little things—spending time with loved ones, enjoying nature, or pursuing hobbies. Simple living encourages us to savor life's moments rather than rush through them.
3. **Enhanced Creativity**: Simplifying our lives can also enhance creativity. With fewer distractions and commitments, we create space for inspiration and innovation. This newfound freedom allows us to explore our passions, whether it's painting, writing, gardening, or any other form of creative expression.
4. **Deeper Connections**: Simple living encourages us to prioritize meaningful relationships. When we reduce our commitments and simplify our lives, we can invest more time and energy into nurturing our connections with family and friends. These deeper relationships enrich our lives and provide a strong support network.
5. **Sustainability**: Choosing a simpler lifestyle often aligns with sustainable practices. By consuming less and being more mindful of our purchases, we contribute to the health of our planet. Simple living encourages us to seek out local and sustainable products, reducing our carbon footprint and promoting a more eco-friendly lifestyle.

Practical Steps to Embrace Simple Living

Incorporating simple living into our lives doesn't have to be an overwhelming endeavor. Here are some practical steps to help you embrace simplicity:

1. **Declutter Your Space**: Start by evaluating your physical possessions. Identify items that no longer serve a purpose or bring you joy. Donate, sell, or recycle these items to create a more organized and peaceful environment. A decluttered space can lead to a decluttered mind.
2. **Simplify Your Schedule**: Take a close look at your commitments and activities. Are there obligations that drain your energy or don't align with your values? Consider prioritizing the activities that truly matter to you and let go of those that don't contribute to your happiness.
3. **Practice Mindfulness**: Incorporate mindfulness practices into your daily routine. This could involve meditation, deep breathing exercises, or simply taking a few moments to appreciate your surroundings. Being present in the moment helps you cultivate gratitude and joy for what you have.
4. **Focus on Experiences**: Shift your focus from material possessions to experiences. Invest time and resources in creating meaningful memories with loved ones. Whether it's a weekend trip, a picnic in the park, or a cooking class, these experiences foster joy and connection that far outweigh the fleeting satisfaction of material goods.
5. **Create a Gratitude Journal**: Keeping a gratitude journal can help you appreciate the simple joys in life. Each day, write down three things you are grateful for, no matter how small. This practice shifts your focus from what you lack to what you have, promoting a sense of contentment.
6. **Limit Digital Distractions**: In our technology-driven world, it's easy to become overwhelmed by constant notifications and information overload. Set boundaries for your screen time and social media usage. Designate specific times for checking emails and social media, and prioritize face-to-face interactions instead.
7. **Embrace Nature**: Spend time outdoors and reconnect with nature. Whether it's a walk in the park, a hike in the woods, or simply enjoying your backyard, nature has a way of grounding us and reminding us of life's simple pleasures.
8. **Nurture Your Passions**: Identify activities that bring you joy and fulfillment. Whether it's painting, writing, gardening, or any other passion, carve out time in your schedule to pursue these interests.

Engaging in what you love adds richness to your life and helps you embrace simplicity.

Cultivating a Mindset of Simplicity

Beyond the practical steps, cultivating a mindset of simplicity is essential for fully embracing this lifestyle. This involves letting go of societal pressures and expectations, allowing yourself the freedom to define what simplicity means for you. Acknowledge that simplicity is a journey, not a destination; it's about making conscious choices that align with your values and priorities.

Being intentional about your choices can lead to a more fulfilling life. This may involve reevaluating your goals and aspirations, focusing on what truly resonates with you. By aligning your actions with your values, you create a sense of purpose that enhances your overall sense of well-being.

The joy of simple living lies in its ability to transform our lives in profound ways. By embracing simplicity, we can reduce stress, cultivate happiness, enhance creativity, and deepen our connections with others. Simple living invites us to appreciate the beauty of everyday moments, shifting our focus from the noise of modern life to the richness of our experiences. As we embark on this journey, let us remember that simplicity is not about deprivation but about making room for what truly matters. By integrating simple living into our daily lives, we can create a more meaningful, fulfilling existence that celebrates the joy found in the ordinary.

Finding Contentment in the Present Moment

In our fast-paced world, where the next goal, deadline, or achievement often dominates our thoughts, the concept of finding contentment in the present moment may seem elusive. Many of us find ourselves constantly chasing future aspirations or dwelling on past experiences, which can lead to feelings of dissatisfaction and anxiety. However, the practice of embracing the present moment can significantly enhance our well-being and sense of fulfillment. By cultivating mindfulness and appreciating the here and now, we can discover true contentment and lead richer, more meaningful lives.

Understanding Contentment

Contentment is a state of mind that encompasses feelings of satisfaction, acceptance, and peace. It is not about complacency or settling for less; rather, it is an acknowledgment of our current circumstances while appreciating the present. This acceptance allows us to let go of the incessant need for more—more success, more possessions, more validation—and find joy in what we already have.

Finding contentment in the present moment is deeply connected to the practice of mindfulness, which involves paying attention to our thoughts, feelings, and sensations without judgment. Mindfulness encourages us to engage fully with our experiences, fostering a sense of appreciation and presence that can lead to profound shifts in our overall outlook.

The Importance of Mindfulness

Mindfulness has gained significant attention in recent years, particularly for its mental health benefits. Research indicates that practicing mindfulness can reduce symptoms of anxiety and depression, improve emotional regulation, and enhance overall well-being. By training our minds to focus on the present, we can break free from the cycle of rumination and worry that often plagues our thoughts.

1. **Cultivating Awareness**: Mindfulness helps us cultivate awareness of our thoughts and feelings, allowing us to recognize when we are caught in the web of future worries or past regrets. By bringing our attention back to the present, we can create a space for reflection and acceptance.
2. **Enhancing Gratitude**: Practicing mindfulness encourages gratitude for the little things we often overlook. When we take the time to notice the beauty of a sunset, the warmth of a cup of tea, or the laughter of a friend, we foster a sense of appreciation that contributes to our overall contentment.
3. **Reducing Stress**: Being present can significantly reduce stress levels. When we focus on the here and now, we become less overwhelmed by the pressures of the future or the weight of the past. This shift in perspective can lead to a more relaxed and peaceful state of mind.
4. **Improving Relationships**: Mindfulness enhances our ability to connect with others. When we are present during conversations, we listen more deeply and engage authentically, fostering stronger relationships and a sense of belonging.

Practical Strategies for Finding Contentment

Finding contentment in the present moment requires practice and intention. Here are several strategies to help you cultivate this mindset:

1. **Mindful Breathing**: One of the simplest ways to anchor yourself in the present is through mindful breathing. Take a few moments each day to focus on your breath. Inhale deeply through your nose, allowing your abdomen to expand, and then exhale slowly through your mouth. As you breathe, pay attention to the sensations in your body, the rhythm of your breath, and the present moment. This practice can help ground you and bring your awareness back to the now.
2. **Engage Your Senses**: Use your senses to enhance your awareness of the present moment. Take time to notice the sights, sounds, smells, and textures around you. Whether you're enjoying a meal, walking in nature, or simply sitting in your living room, consciously engage with your environment. This sensory awareness fosters a deeper connection to the present.
3. **Practice Gratitude**: Incorporating gratitude into your daily routine can significantly shift your perspective. Each day, take a few moments to reflect on what you are grateful for. This could be as simple as appreciating the warmth of the sun on your skin or the comfort of your home. By recognizing and expressing gratitude for the present moment, you cultivate a sense of contentment.
4. **Limit Multitasking**: In our digital age, multitasking has become the norm, often leading to feelings of overwhelm. Instead, focus on one task at a time. Whether it's eating, working, or spending time with loved ones, give your full attention to the task at hand. This practice not only enhances your effectiveness but also allows you to savor each moment fully.
5. **Create a Mindful Ritual**: Establishing a daily ritual can help you anchor your awareness in the present. This could be a morning coffee routine, a nightly reflection on your day, or an evening walk. Incorporating mindfulness into these rituals can deepen your sense of contentment and provide a moment of peace in your day.
6. **Limit Social Media**: While social media can be a way to connect, it can also lead to comparison and dissatisfaction. Consider setting boundaries around your social media use to prevent distractions from the present moment. Instead of scrolling through feeds, engage with the people and activities around you.
7. **Embrace Imperfection**: Finding contentment in the present requires letting go of perfectionism. Accept that life is not always tidy and that challenges are a part of the journey. Embracing imperfection allows you

to appreciate the beauty in the messy, unpredictable moments of life.

The Power of Acceptance

One of the core principles of finding contentment in the present moment is acceptance. Acceptance does not mean resignation or passivity; rather, it is the acknowledgment of reality as it is. When we accept our current circumstances—whether they involve challenges or joys—we free ourselves from the burden of constant striving.

Acceptance opens the door to peace and contentment. Instead of resisting what is, we can embrace the present moment with open arms. This shift in perspective allows us to respond to life's challenges with grace and resilience, ultimately leading to greater emotional stability.

Finding contentment in the present moment is a journey that requires mindfulness, intention, and practice. By cultivating awareness, engaging our senses, and embracing gratitude, we can enhance our ability to appreciate the beauty of everyday life. Simple practices, such as mindful breathing and limiting distractions, can significantly shift our perspectives and help us find joy in the here and now. Ultimately, contentment is not a destination but a way of being—an invitation to savor life's fleeting moments and recognize the abundance that exists within us and around us. By embracing the present, we unlock the door to a more fulfilling and enriched life, where every moment is an opportunity for joy and connection.

TWELVE

Redefining Success and Happiness

In today's world, success and happiness are often measured by external markers such as wealth, status, and achievements. Society frequently equates success with high-paying jobs, material possessions, or recognition, and happiness with the attainment of these goals. However, this conventional definition leaves many feeling unfulfilled, leading to an increasing desire to redefine what success and happiness truly mean. Redefining these concepts requires a shift from external validation to internal satisfaction, prioritizing well-being, purpose, and contentment over societal expectations.

The Traditional Notion of Success

Historically, success has been linked to the accumulation of wealth, power, and prestige. From an early age, people are encouraged to set goals that align with career advancement, financial prosperity, and social status. This traditional notion is reinforced by cultural norms, the media, and the expectations of those around us, creating a standard of success that is largely based on comparison with others.

While striving for these forms of success can lead to professional achievement, they often come at a personal cost. Many individuals who achieve societal markers of success still experience feelings of emptiness or dissatisfaction. This disillusionment can occur because traditional success tends to focus on external validation rather than internal fulfillment. When people define their self-worth by their job title or bank balance, they risk neglecting the deeper aspects of their well-being—such as emotional, psychological, and spiritual health.

Redefining Success

To redefine success, it's important to shift from an external focus to an internal one. True success is not about conforming to societal expectations or achieving specific milestones; it's about finding personal meaning and fulfillment in life. Redefining success involves aligning your goals and actions with your core values and passions, rather than chasing external approval.

1. **Aligning with Purpose**: A critical aspect of redefining success is identifying your purpose. When people live in alignment with their purpose, they experience a sense of meaning and direction that transcends material achievements. Your purpose might involve contributing to your community, pursuing a creative passion, or fostering meaningful relationships. Defining success in terms of purpose allows you to live a life that feels authentic and satisfying, regardless of external recognition.
2. **Fostering Well-Being**: Redefining success also means prioritizing your overall well-being. Mental, emotional, and physical health are integral to a fulfilling life. Success should not come at the expense of your health; instead, it should enhance your quality of life. Balancing work with self-care, rest, and personal development is key to achieving a holistic sense of success.
3. **Building Meaningful Relationships**: Another way to redefine success is by placing more value on relationships. Deep connections with family, friends, and colleagues often bring a sense of joy and satisfaction that material success cannot. Strong relationships contribute to emotional support, trust, and a sense of belonging, all of which are essential to long-term happiness.
4. **Pursuing Passion and Creativity**: Success is also about engaging in activities that bring you joy and fulfillment. Whether it's pursuing a hobby, developing new skills, or engaging in creative endeavors, these pursuits foster a sense of accomplishment that comes from within. Redefining success in this way encourages you to focus on what makes you feel alive, rather than what society deems important.
5. **Embracing Lifelong Learning**: Viewing success as a lifelong journey of growth and learning can lead to a more fulfilling life. Success doesn't have to be measured by a finite endpoint; instead, it can be seen as an ongoing process of personal and professional development. Embracing new experiences and challenges, even when they don't lead to traditional achievements, can contribute to a deeper sense of purpose and satisfaction.

The Traditional Notion of Happiness

Much like success, happiness is often defined in external terms. People are frequently told that happiness comes from the attainment of goals, possessions, or experiences—whether it's buying a new car, landing a promotion, or traveling to exotic destinations. However, this external pursuit of happiness can be fleeting. While these experiences may bring temporary joy, they do not provide lasting fulfillment.

Moreover, the societal pressure to constantly chase happiness can create a sense of inadequacy when we don't feel perpetually joyful. The expectation that happiness should be a constant state leads to the misconception that any negative emotion is a sign of failure, which prevents us from experiencing the full range of human emotions.

Redefining Happiness

Redefining happiness involves shifting away from the pursuit of fleeting pleasures and instead focusing on cultivating inner peace, gratitude, and contentment. True happiness is not dependent on external circumstances but is a state of being that comes from within. It is about embracing the present moment, finding joy in simplicity, and accepting life's ups and downs with grace.

1. **Contentment Over Achievement**: Redefining happiness involves recognizing that contentment is not tied to achieving specific goals. While achievements can contribute to feelings of accomplishment, lasting happiness comes from appreciating the present moment and finding joy in everyday experiences. Cultivating gratitude for what you have, rather than focusing on what you lack, fosters a sense of contentment that is more sustainable than the pursuit of external rewards.
2. **Embracing Imperfection**: Happiness is not about the absence of difficulties but about how we navigate them. Accepting that life is imperfect allows us to experience happiness even in challenging times. Redefining happiness means letting go of the idea that we need to be happy all the time and instead embracing a more balanced emotional life.
3. **Practicing Mindfulness**: Mindfulness plays a crucial role in redefining happiness. By being fully present in the moment, we can savor life's simple pleasures and connect more deeply with our surroundings. Whether it's enjoying a meal, taking a walk, or spending time with loved

ones, mindfulness helps us appreciate the richness of our experiences, which leads to a more profound sense of happiness.

4. **Fostering Compassion**: Happiness is often tied to our relationships with others. Cultivating compassion and kindness toward others can significantly enhance our own happiness. Acts of kindness and empathy not only improve the well-being of others but also contribute to our own sense of purpose and fulfillment.
5. **Letting Go of Comparison**: One of the barriers to happiness is the tendency to compare ourselves to others. Redefining happiness involves letting go of comparison and focusing on your own path. Everyone's journey is unique, and finding happiness means embracing your own experiences, rather than measuring them against someone else's.

Redefining success and happiness requires a shift in perspective, from external validation to internal fulfillment. Success is not about wealth or status, but about living in alignment with your values, purpose, and passions. Similarly, happiness is not about the pursuit of perfection or the attainment of material goods, but about finding contentment in the present moment, embracing life's imperfections, and cultivating gratitude. By redefining these concepts, we can create more meaningful, authentic lives that prioritize well-being, relationships, and personal growth over societal expectations.

Finding Joy in the Journey, Not the Destination

In modern society, much of our focus is on achieving goals, reaching milestones, and attaining success. We're often taught that happiness lies in the future, waiting for us at the end of a project, a promotion, or a personal achievement. However, in the pursuit of these goals, we may overlook the value of the journey itself. Finding joy in the journey, rather than focusing solely on the destination, is a mindset shift that can lead to a more fulfilling, balanced, and joyful life.

The Trap of Destination Happiness

The notion of destination happiness is ingrained in many of us from a young age. We are encouraged to set goals, work hard, and expect happiness as a reward once we achieve them. Whether it's graduating from school, getting a dream job, buying a house, or reaching a fitness goal, these accomplishments are often viewed as the end point where happiness awaits. However, this perspective can create a cycle of perpetual striving, where each achievement is followed by another goal, leaving little room for true contentment.

The problem with destination happiness is that it places fulfillment in the future, constantly postponing joy until the next big accomplishment. This mindset can lead to a sense of emptiness when the goal is achieved, as the excitement fades quickly and a new pursuit takes its place. As a result, many people feel a sense of dissatisfaction despite outward success because they haven't learned to appreciate the process leading up to their achievements.

Embracing the Journey

Finding joy in the journey means appreciating the present moment, embracing the process of growth, and recognizing the value of everyday experiences. It's about shifting the focus from the end goal to the path we take to get there. This approach encourages us to live more mindfully, savor each step along the way, and find meaning in the small victories, challenges, and lessons that arise throughout the journey.

1. **Focusing on Growth, Not Perfection**

When we concentrate solely on reaching a particular goal, we may miss the opportunity to learn and grow during the process. The journey is where growth happens—where we develop new skills, overcome challenges, and build resilience. By embracing the journey, we learn to value progress over perfection and recognize that the process of self-improvement is often more rewarding than the achievement itself.

In personal development, for example, the journey might involve setting a goal to become more confident or emotionally intelligent. Rather than fixating on when you will finally "arrive" at this version of yourself, you can find joy in each small step that brings you closer to your goal—whether it's practicing self-compassion, learning from setbacks, or simply becoming more aware of your emotions.

1. **Building Meaningful Connections**

The journey often involves connecting with others, whether in the workplace, social settings, or personal relationships. When we are focused only on the destination, we may miss the opportunity to build and nurture these connections. Relationships are a significant part of life, and finding joy in the journey often means cherishing the time spent with those around us—collaborating with colleagues, sharing experiences with friends, or growing closer to family.

By valuing the journey, we can focus on fostering deeper, more meaningful connections with the people we encounter along the way. These relationships often provide support, encouragement, and companionship, enriching our lives and making the journey more enjoyable.

3. **Appreciating the Small Wins**

Every journey is filled with small victories that deserve recognition. Whether it's mastering a new skill, overcoming a fear, or simply taking one step closer to a larger goal, these moments are worth celebrating. Focusing on these small wins can provide a sense of accomplishment and motivation, helping us stay engaged and joyful throughout the process.

For example, if your goal is to write a book, finding joy in the journey might mean celebrating each chapter completed or appreciating the insights gained through the research process. These small victories remind us that progress is being made, even if the final goal is still far off.

4. **Living in the Present Moment**

One of the most powerful aspects of finding joy in the journey is learning to live in the present moment. When we are constantly focused on future goals, we often neglect the beauty of the present. Mindfulness teaches us to be fully engaged in the here and now, to appreciate the sights, sounds, and experiences of each moment without judgment.

Practicing mindfulness during the journey can transform ordinary moments into sources of joy. Whether it's savoring a quiet morning with a cup of coffee, enjoying a walk in nature, or fully immersing yourself in a task at work, being present allows you to experience life more deeply and fully. The journey becomes richer and more fulfilling when we allow ourselves to slow down and appreciate each moment as it unfolds.

5. **Learning from Setbacks**

The journey is rarely a straight line. It's filled with obstacles, setbacks, and detours that can test our patience and perseverance. While these challenges may seem frustrating at the time, they are also opportunities for growth and learning. Finding joy in the journey means embracing these challenges as valuable parts of the experience, rather than viewing them as distractions from the end goal.

Setbacks teach us resilience, adaptability, and problem-solving skills. They force us to reevaluate our strategies, develop new approaches, and build mental toughness. When we learn to see obstacles as opportunities for growth, the journey becomes more rewarding, and we become more equipped to handle future challenges with grace.

6. **Reevaluating Success**

Redefining success is another important aspect of finding joy in the journey. Success is not solely about reaching a particular destination; it's also about how we live along the way. When we focus only on achieving a specific outcome, we may neglect the qualities that make the journey meaningful—such as integrity, kindness, creativity, and passion.

By redefining success as the ability to stay true to our values, pursue what we love, and maintain balance in our lives, we can find joy in the everyday actions that lead us toward our goals. Success, in this sense, is not just about the final result but about living in alignment with who we are and what we stand for.

Finding joy in the journey is a powerful shift in mindset that allows us to live more fully and meaningfully. By focusing on growth, appreciating the present moment, and embracing the challenges along the way, we can cultivate a sense of fulfillment that goes beyond the destination. The journey itself is where life happens—it's where we learn, connect, and evolve. When we find joy in the process, rather than fixating solely on the outcome, we create a richer, more rewarding experience that enhances our overall happiness and well-being.

Living a Life Aligned with Your True Self

Living a life aligned with your true self means leading an authentic existence based on your core values, beliefs, passions, and inner desires. It involves embracing your individuality and making choices that reflect who you truly are rather than conforming to societal expectations or external pressures. This journey toward self-alignment fosters deeper fulfillment, inner peace, and long-lasting happiness, as it empowers you to live with integrity and purpose.

Understanding the True Self

The "true self" refers to the authentic, unfiltered version of who you are—your unique combination of qualities, beliefs, desires, and potential. It is the essence of your being that is often hidden beneath layers of societal conditioning, expectations from others, and self-imposed limitations. Many people spend much of their lives disconnected from their true selves because they prioritize pleasing others, meeting societal standards, or adhering to cultural norms that may not resonate with them.

Understanding and connecting with your true self requires introspection, self-awareness, and a willingness to explore your innermost thoughts and emotions. It involves shedding the masks you wear to fit in or gain approval and instead embracing who you are at your core. This process is deeply personal and ongoing, as people evolve and grow throughout their lives.

The Consequences of Living Out of Alignment

When you live out of alignment with your true self, you may experience feelings of discontent, restlessness, or even emptiness. You might find yourself going through the motions of life without feeling truly connected to your actions or decisions. This misalignment can manifest in various ways:

1. **Disconnection**: When you are not aligned with your true self, there is often a disconnect between your internal desires and your external actions. This can lead to a sense of inner conflict, where you feel torn between what you truly want and what you believe is expected of you. Over time, this disconnection can contribute to feelings of frustration, dissatisfaction, or lack of purpose.
2. **Living for Others**: Many people fall into the trap of living for others, whether it's family, friends, or society at large. While it's natural to want to meet the expectations of those around you, constantly prioritizing others' desires over your own can cause you to lose sight of your true self. You may end up pursuing goals or living a lifestyle that doesn't align with your passions or values, which can lead to long-term unhappiness.
3. **Emotional Discomfort**: Living out of alignment often creates emotional discomfort, such as anxiety, stress, or depression. This discomfort arises from the tension between who you are and who you are pretending to be. When you suppress your true self, it becomes harder to feel authentic happiness, as your life may not reflect what genuinely fulfills you.
4. **Lack of Fulfillment**: No matter how much external success or recognition you achieve, if your life is not aligned with your true self,

you may struggle to find lasting fulfillment. Even after reaching career milestones or acquiring material wealth, the sense of inner emptiness may persist, as these accomplishments don't resonate with your deeper needs or aspirations.

The Benefits of Living Aligned with Your True Self

On the other hand, living in alignment with your true self brings numerous benefits that contribute to your overall well-being, happiness, and sense of purpose. By embracing your authenticity, you are better able to create a life that is rich with meaning and aligned with your inner desires.

1. **Inner Peace and Contentment**: One of the most significant benefits of living authentically is the sense of inner peace it provides. When your actions, decisions, and lifestyle reflect your true self, you experience less internal conflict and more harmony between your inner and outer worlds. This alignment fosters contentment, as you no longer feel the need to constantly chase approval or validation from others.
2. **Clarity and Direction**: When you are in tune with your true self, you gain clarity about what you truly want in life. This sense of clarity allows you to make decisions with confidence, as you are guided by your core values and inner compass. Rather than feeling uncertain or swayed by external influences, you are empowered to pursue paths that align with your unique passions and purpose.
3. **Increased Self-Confidence**: Living in alignment with your true self builds self-confidence, as you become more comfortable with who you are. When you stop trying to be someone you're not, you free yourself from the burden of comparison or self-doubt. Embracing your individuality allows you to stand firmly in your truth, knowing that your worth comes from within, not from external validation.
4. **Deeper Relationships**: Authenticity fosters deeper, more meaningful connections with others. When you live in alignment with your true self, you attract relationships based on mutual understanding, respect, and shared values. These relationships are more fulfilling because they are built on honesty and trust, rather than on superficial appearances or societal expectations. Additionally, living authentically encourages those around you to do the same, fostering a supportive and empowering community.

5. **Greater Fulfillment**: Ultimately, living in alignment with your true self leads to a greater sense of fulfillment in all areas of life. Whether it's in your career, relationships, or personal pursuits, when you are true to yourself, you experience a deeper connection to your purpose. Fulfillment comes not from external achievements but from knowing that you are living a life that reflects your authentic desires and passions.

Steps to Living Aligned with Your True Self

Living a life aligned with your true self is an ongoing process that requires self-reflection, courage, and commitment. It involves making conscious choices that honor your authenticity, even when it challenges societal norms or expectations. Here are some steps to help you live in alignment with your true self:

1. **Practice Self-Awareness**: The first step to living authentically is to cultivate self-awareness. Take time to reflect on your thoughts, feelings, values, and desires. Journaling, meditation, or speaking with a trusted friend or therapist can help you gain deeper insights into who you are and what you truly want. Identify any areas of your life where you feel disconnected from your true self and explore what changes might bring you closer to alignment.
2. **Let Go of Societal Expectations**: One of the most challenging aspects of living authentically is releasing the need to conform to societal expectations. This may involve questioning long-held beliefs about success, happiness, or what it means to live a "good" life. Remember that everyone's path is unique, and living in alignment with your true self may mean breaking away from traditional norms or redefining what success looks like for you.
3. **Embrace Vulnerability**: Living authentically requires a willingness to be vulnerable. This means being open about who you are, even if it means facing criticism or rejection. Vulnerability is a strength that allows you to connect more deeply with others and live with greater integrity. Embrace the courage it takes to be true to yourself, knowing that authenticity is far more rewarding than living a life of pretense.
4. **Set Boundaries**: Living in alignment with your true self also involves setting boundaries with others. Learn to say no to things that don't serve your well-being or align with your values. Setting healthy boundaries protects your time, energy, and emotional health, allowing you to stay

true to yourself and your priorities.

5. **Pursue What Lights You Up**: Follow your passions and engage in activities that bring you joy and fulfillment. Whether it's a creative hobby, a meaningful career, or a personal pursuit, prioritize the things that align with your true self. By doing what you love, you not only enhance your own happiness but also contribute to the world in a way that feels authentic and impactful.

Living a life aligned with your true self is a journey of self-discovery, authenticity, and inner growth. It requires courage to break free from societal expectations and embrace who you truly are. However, the rewards are profound—greater fulfillment, deeper connections, and a sense of inner peace that comes from living a life that reflects your true essence. When you align your actions, decisions, and lifestyle with your true self, you create a life that is rich with meaning, purpose, and joy.

THIRTEEN

Part V: Lessons on Giving Back

The Ripple Effect of Kindness

Kindness is one of the most powerful forces in human interaction, capable of transforming individuals, communities, and even the world. Acts of kindness, whether small or large, have a ripple effect, meaning they extend beyond the initial gesture to influence others in unexpected ways. The beauty of kindness lies in its simplicity—anyone can perform an act of kindness, and its effects can multiply as it touches the lives of others. The ripple effect of kindness demonstrates how one good deed can create a cascade of positive outcomes, not only for the recipient but also for the giver and even those who observe it.

The Science Behind Kindness

Kindness is not only a moral virtue; it is deeply rooted in human psychology and biology. Studies have shown that performing or receiving acts of kindness can trigger the release of "feel-good" hormones, such as oxytocin, serotonin, and dopamine. These chemicals are responsible for feelings of happiness, contentment, and well-being. Additionally, oxytocin, often referred to as the "love hormone," can enhance bonding and trust between individuals. This means that kindness has a biological basis for promoting positive social interactions and fostering stronger relationships.

Furthermore, research has shown that witnessing acts of kindness can lead to what is known as "elevation," a warm feeling of inspiration and admiration. Elevation can motivate people to perform their own acts of kindness, further extending the ripple effect. This suggests that kindness is contagious—it inspires others to spread compassion, empathy, and generosity.

The Immediate Impact of Kindness

When someone performs an act of kindness, the immediate impact is often visible in the recipient's reaction. Simple gestures like helping someone carry groceries, offering a genuine compliment, or donating to a charitable cause can brighten a person's day and shift their mood from negative to positive. In many cases, recipients of kindness experience a sense of relief, joy, or gratitude. These feelings can have a profound impact on their emotional and mental well-being, helping them to feel valued, supported, and less alone in the world.

For example, imagine a person who is struggling through a difficult day and feeling overwhelmed. A kind word or gesture from a stranger might lift their spirits, reminding them that they are not invisible or isolated. This seemingly small act of kindness could give them the strength to continue facing their challenges and may even inspire them to pass the kindness forward to someone else.

The Ripple Effect in Communities

Kindness also plays a critical role in strengthening communities and creating a sense of social cohesion. When individuals in a community engage in acts of kindness, they build trust, empathy, and cooperation among members. These qualities are essential for fostering a sense of belonging and mutual support within the community. Over time, a culture of kindness can lead to more compassionate and inclusive communities where people feel safe and cared for.

For instance, in a neighborhood where residents are kind and helpful to one another, there is likely to be a greater sense of solidarity and mutual respect. Neighbors may look out for one another, share resources, or offer assistance during times of need. This creates a supportive environment where individuals feel more connected and invested in the well-being of others. The ripple effect of kindness, in this context, helps to create a community where people are motivated to work together for the common good.

One real-world example of the ripple effect of kindness in communities can be seen in the "pay-it-forward" phenomenon. This occurs when someone receives an act of kindness, such as having their coffee paid for by a stranger, and decides to "pay it forward" by doing the same for someone else. Over time, this chain of kindness can grow, impacting dozens or even hundreds of people. Such acts of generosity can serve as a reminder that even small, simple gestures can have a lasting impact.

Kindness in the Workplace

The ripple effect of kindness extends beyond personal and community relationships; it also plays a vital role in the workplace. A positive work environment, where kindness is encouraged and practiced, leads to higher levels of employee engagement, satisfaction, and productivity. Acts of kindness in the workplace—such as offering to help a colleague with a project, providing constructive feedback with empathy, or acknowledging someone's hard work—can reduce stress and foster a sense of teamwork.

When leaders demonstrate kindness, it sets the tone for the entire organization. Employees who feel valued and respected are more likely to be motivated, loyal, and committed to their work. Furthermore, kindness can reduce conflicts in the workplace, as it encourages open communication and mutual understanding. In this way, the ripple effect of kindness can contribute to a healthier, more harmonious work environment, where collaboration and support thrive.

Kindness and Its Impact on Mental Health

In addition to its social benefits, kindness also has a significant impact on mental health. Both giving and receiving kindness can boost self-esteem, reduce feelings of isolation, and alleviate symptoms of depression and anxiety. When you practice kindness, you engage in behaviors that reaffirm your sense of purpose and worth, which can lead to greater emotional resilience and overall well-being.

For individuals struggling with mental health issues, experiencing kindness can serve as a reminder that they are not alone and that others care about their well-being. This can provide a powerful sense of connection and hope, which may encourage them to seek help or reach out to others for support.

Moreover, acts of self-kindness—such as practicing self-care, setting healthy boundaries, and treating oneself with compassion—are essential for maintaining good mental health. By extending kindness to yourself, you create a foundation of self-love and acceptance that enables you to better cope with life's challenges. In turn, this self-kindness empowers you to spread kindness to others, continuing the ripple effect.

Kindness as a Catalyst for Social Change

On a larger scale, the ripple effect of kindness can be a catalyst for social change. Acts of kindness, when multiplied, have the potential to create shifts in societal attitudes and behaviors. For instance, movements such as Random Acts of Kindness Day or Pay It Forward campaigns encourage individuals to engage in acts of kindness with the understanding that these actions can influence broader social norms.

When kindness becomes a cultural value, it can lead to more compassionate policies, inclusive practices, and a greater emphasis on social justice. Consider the role that kindness plays in humanitarian efforts, community service, and volunteerism. These efforts often start with the intention of helping others in need, but their impact extends far beyond immediate relief. Over time, such actions contribute to a more equitable and empathetic society, where individuals are motivated to work toward the well-being of all people.

Conclusion: The Ever-Expanding Reach of Kindness

The ripple effect of kindness is a testament to the profound and far-reaching impact that simple acts of compassion can have on the world. Whether it's a small gesture of kindness to a stranger or a significant act of generosity to a community, the effects of kindness can extend far beyond the initial act. It spreads from person to person, inspiring others to be kind in turn and creating a chain reaction of positivity and goodwill.

In a world that often feels divided or chaotic, kindness serves as a unifying force, reminding us of our shared humanity and the power we have to make a difference. As we cultivate kindness in our daily lives—toward ourselves, others, and the world—we contribute to a more compassionate, just, and connected world. By understanding the ripple effect of kindness, we can recognize the potential within each of us to create positive change, one kind act at a time.

Giving Without Expecting in Return

Giving without expecting anything in return is one of the most selfless acts a person can perform. It signifies a deep sense of generosity and compassion, where the act of giving is its own reward. This mindset transcends transactional exchanges and highlights the essence of human kindness. When people give without anticipation of reciprocation, they foster a culture of care, inspire goodwill, and contribute to a more compassionate world. The beauty of this type of giving lies in its authenticity—it stems from a genuine desire to help others, not from the hope of gaining something in return.

The Nature of Altruism

Altruism is often defined as the selfless concern for the well-being of others. It's a concept that has been discussed by philosophers, psychologists, and religious leaders for centuries. True altruism involves acting with the intention of benefiting another person, without any expectation of personal gain. This is the foundation of giving without expecting in return.

Human beings are social creatures, and acts of kindness and generosity are essential for building and maintaining healthy relationships. However, in many cases, acts of kindness are driven by a sense of reciprocity—the idea that if we give something, we will receive something in return. While there is nothing inherently wrong with reciprocal exchanges, altruistic giving requires us to go a step further. It challenges us to act without expecting recognition, rewards, or payback. Altruism asks us to give simply because it is the right thing to do.

The Emotional Benefits of Giving Selflessly

One might think that giving without receiving would be emotionally exhausting, but research shows that selfless giving is highly beneficial for the giver. Studies have found that acts of altruism can increase happiness, reduce stress, and enhance overall well-being. This phenomenon, often referred to as the "helper's high," is the result of feel-good chemicals, such as endorphins and oxytocin, being released in the brain when we perform acts of kindness.

When we give without expecting anything in return, we cultivate a sense of inner satisfaction and fulfillment. The joy of seeing someone else benefit from our actions creates a deep sense of purpose and meaning. It reinforces our connection to others and reminds us of our ability to make a positive impact in the world.

Moreover, selfless giving can strengthen our sense of empathy. By putting ourselves in the shoes of others, we develop a deeper understanding of their needs and challenges. This fosters compassion and allows us to approach life with greater humility and awareness.

Creating a Ripple Effect

One of the most powerful aspects of giving without expecting anything in return is its potential to create a ripple effect. When someone experiences an act of kindness, they are often inspired to pay it forward. This sets off a chain reaction of generosity and goodwill that can spread far beyond the original act.

For example, imagine paying for a stranger's coffee. That small act of kindness could brighten their day and inspire them to do something kind for someone else. In this way, a single act of selflessness has the potential to multiply, touching the lives of countless people.

This ripple effect is not only beneficial for individuals; it also strengthens communities. When people give freely and without expectation, they contribute to a culture of care and support. Communities where altruism is practiced tend to be more cohesive, resilient, and inclusive. People are more likely to trust and help one another, creating a positive cycle of kindness and cooperation.

Letting Go of Expectations

One of the biggest challenges in giving without expecting anything in return is learning to let go of expectations. In our modern, transactional society, it's easy to fall into the habit of measuring our actions based on what we will receive in return. This mindset can be limiting, as it places a condition on our generosity.

To practice true altruism, we must let go of the need for recognition, gratitude, or reciprocation. This doesn't mean that we shouldn't appreciate a "thank you" or feel good when someone acknowledges our efforts. Rather, it means that our primary motivation for giving should come from a genuine desire to help, rather than from the hope of receiving something in return.

Letting go of expectations can be difficult, especially if we have been conditioned to expect something in exchange for our efforts. However, with practice, it becomes easier to embrace a mindset of abundance and selflessness. By focusing on the joy of giving rather than on what we stand to gain, we free ourselves from the limitations of transactional thinking.

Overcoming the Fear of Being Taken Advantage Of

One common concern about giving without expecting in return is the fear of being taken advantage of. People may worry that if they give too much without expecting anything in return, others will exploit their generosity. While this is a valid concern, it's important to remember that giving selflessly does not mean allowing others to take advantage of us.

Boundaries are essential in any act of giving. It's important to be generous, but it's also important to protect our own well-being and ensure that we are not overextending ourselves. Selfless giving should come from a place of abundance and joy, not from a sense of obligation or guilt.

By setting clear boundaries and being mindful of our own needs, we can give freely without fear of being exploited. This allows us to strike a balance between generosity and self-care, ensuring that our acts of kindness are sustainable and genuine.

The Spiritual Dimension of Giving

Many spiritual traditions emphasize the importance of giving without expectation. In Buddhism, the concept of "dāna" refers to the practice of giving freely, without attachment to the outcome. In Christianity, the act of charity is considered one of the highest virtues, and in Hinduism, the principle of "seva" encourages selfless service to others.

These teachings highlight the spiritual dimension of giving. When we give without expecting in return, we tap into a deeper sense of connection with the world around us. We recognize that our actions are part of something larger than ourselves, and we become more attuned to the interconnectedness of all beings.

Giving selflessly can also be a form of meditation or mindfulness. By focusing on the present moment and the act of giving itself, we become more aware of the impact we are making. This awareness can bring a sense of peace and fulfillment, as we realize that we are contributing to the well-being of others in a meaningful way.

The Freedom of Selfless Giving

Giving without expecting in return is a practice that requires intentionality, empathy, and a willingness to let go of our own desires for recognition or reward. It challenges us to step outside of the transactional mindset and embrace a more compassionate, altruistic approach to life.

The benefits of selfless giving are profound—not only for the recipient but also for the giver. It fosters emotional well-being, strengthens relationships, and creates a ripple effect of kindness that can spread throughout communities and beyond. Moreover, selfless giving allows us to tap into a deeper sense of purpose and spiritual fulfillment.

Ultimately, giving without expecting anything in return is a path to true freedom. It liberates us from the constraints of conditional generosity and allows us to experience the joy of giving in its purest form. By practicing selfless giving, we can contribute to a more compassionate and connected world, one act of kindness at a time.

The Joy of Helping Others

Helping others is one of the most fulfilling and joyful experiences a person can have. It brings a sense of purpose, connection, and satisfaction that few other activities can match. Whether it's offering a helping hand to a friend, volunteering in your community, or simply performing small acts of kindness, the joy of helping others is universal. This joy stems from our natural inclination to connect with and support those around us. When we help others, we not only improve their lives but also enrich our own in profound ways.

The Psychological Benefits of Helping Others

When people engage in acts of kindness or help others, they experience a psychological boost that is often referred to as a "helper's high." This feeling comes from the release of neurotransmitters like dopamine and oxytocin in the brain. Dopamine is associated with pleasure and reward, while oxytocin promotes feelings of bonding and trust. Together, these chemicals create a sense of well-being and happiness.

Research has shown that helping others can reduce stress, increase happiness, and improve overall mental health. People who regularly engage in altruistic activities tend to have lower rates of depression and anxiety. Helping others allows us to shift our focus away from our own problems and challenges, which can provide a refreshing sense of perspective. When we see that our actions are making a positive impact on someone else's life, it reinforces our sense of self-worth and gives us a deeper sense of purpose.

Building Stronger Connections

Helping others is also a powerful way to strengthen social connections. Human beings are inherently social creatures, and our sense of belonging and connection to others is a fundamental part of our well-being. When we help someone, we create a bond that can lead to lasting friendships and relationships. These connections not only enrich our lives but also provide a support system that we can rely on in times of need.

The act of helping fosters trust and mutual respect between individuals. Whether it's helping a neighbor, supporting a colleague, or volunteering for a cause, these acts of kindness build a sense of community. When people feel supported and valued, they are more likely to offer help in return, creating a positive cycle of generosity and compassion.

The Ripple Effect of Kindness

One of the most beautiful aspects of helping others is the ripple effect it creates. When someone receives help or experiences an act of kindness, they are often inspired to pay it forward. This sets off a chain reaction of good deeds that can spread far beyond the initial act. In this way, a single act of helping can have a far-reaching impact, touching the lives of many people.

For example, imagine you help a colleague with a difficult project. Your assistance not only alleviates their stress but also encourages them to help others when the opportunity arises. As a result, the positive impact of your help extends beyond just one person—it can inspire an entire network of generosity.

This ripple effect is a powerful reminder that even small acts of kindness can have a significant impact. Whether it's offering a smile to a stranger or donating to a cause, every act of helping has the potential to make the world a better place.

Personal Growth and Self-Discovery

Helping others is not only beneficial for those we assist but also contributes to our personal growth and self-discovery. When we engage in acts of kindness, we often step outside our comfort zones and challenge ourselves to be more compassionate, patient, and understanding. These experiences help us grow as individuals, teaching us valuable lessons about empathy, resilience, and the power of community.

By helping others, we also gain insight into our own strengths and capabilities. We learn that we have the ability to make a difference, no matter how small our actions may seem. This realization can boost our confidence and motivate us to continue contributing to the well-being of those around us.

Moreover, helping others can help us discover new passions and interests. Many people find that volunteering or engaging in charitable activities opens their eyes to causes they feel deeply connected to. This sense of purpose can guide us in making meaningful contributions to society, both in our personal and professional lives.

Enhancing Emotional Well-Being

Helping others is closely linked to emotional well-being. When we focus on assisting those in need, we cultivate a sense of gratitude for what we have in our own lives. This gratitude fosters contentment and reduces feelings of dissatisfaction or envy. By recognizing the struggles of others, we are reminded of our own blessings, which can lead to greater emotional resilience.

Acts of helping also encourage us to be more mindful and present in our daily lives. When we help someone, we are fully engaged in the moment, focusing on their needs rather than our own concerns. This mindfulness can reduce feelings of stress and anxiety, promoting a greater sense of peace and balance.

Additionally, helping others allows us to experience the joy of shared experiences. Whether we are volunteering alongside others or simply offering a kind word to a friend, these moments of connection bring us closer to those around us and remind us of the importance of community.

Helping Without Expectation

One of the key aspects of finding joy in helping others is learning to give without expecting anything in return. This kind of altruistic giving is rooted in the desire to make a positive difference, rather than in the hope of receiving recognition or reward. When we help others without expecting anything in return, we experience a purer form of joy, unclouded by the need for validation or reciprocation.

This mindset also frees us from disappointment or frustration when our efforts are not immediately acknowledged or reciprocated. By focusing on the act of helping itself, rather than on the outcome, we can find satisfaction in knowing that we have done something good, regardless of how it is received.

The Role of Compassion and Empathy

Compassion and empathy are central to the joy of helping others. When we truly understand and connect with the struggles of those around us, we are more motivated to offer help and support. Empathy allows us to put ourselves in someone else's shoes and imagine how we would feel in their situation. This understanding fosters a deep sense of compassion, which in turn drives us to take action.

Compassionate helping is not about pity or condescension, but rather about recognizing our shared humanity. It's about acknowledging that we are all in this together, and that by lifting others up, we are also lifting ourselves.

The Enduring Joy of Helping

Helping others brings joy not only to those we assist but also to ourselves. It strengthens our social connections, enhances our emotional well-being, and fosters personal growth. Acts of kindness, whether big or small, create a ripple effect that can spread throughout our communities, inspiring others to give and contribute to a culture of care.

Ultimately, the joy of helping others comes from the recognition that we are all interconnected, and that by giving freely, we are enriching not just the lives of others but also our own. In a world that can sometimes feel divided, helping others is a powerful reminder of the strength of compassion, empathy, and human connection.

Chapter 13: Legacy and Impact

How Your Actions Affect Others

Every action we take, no matter how small or significant, has an impact on the people around us. This effect can be direct or indirect, immediate or long-term, but it is undeniable that our behaviors shape the environment and influence others in ways we may not always realize. Understanding how our actions affect others can lead to more thoughtful, compassionate decision-making and foster positive relationships in both personal and professional settings.

The Ripple Effect of Actions

One of the most profound ways our actions affect others is through the ripple effect. Much like a stone dropped into a pond creates ripples that spread outward, our actions influence not only the people directly involved but also those they interact with. For example, a single act of kindness—like offering help to a colleague—can inspire that person to act kindly towards others, creating a chain of positivity that extends beyond the initial interaction.

Conversely, negative actions can have a ripple effect as well. A harsh word or rude gesture can leave someone feeling upset or unappreciated, which may cause them to carry those negative emotions into their other interactions. This chain reaction can result in tension or misunderstandings, affecting the overall atmosphere of a group or community.

Impact on Emotional Well-Being

Our actions have a significant impact on the emotional well-being of others. Positive actions, such as offering support, listening with empathy, or expressing gratitude, can uplift someone's mood and foster a sense of belonging and connection. These small gestures can make people feel valued and appreciated, which in turn boosts their confidence and mental health.

On the other hand, negative behaviors—such as criticism, neglect, or selfishness—can diminish someone's emotional well-being. When we are unkind or dismissive, it can hurt others, lower their self-esteem, or make them feel isolated. Recognizing how our actions can affect someone's emotional state encourages us to act with more care, fostering an environment of mutual respect and understanding.

Building or Breaking Trust

Trust is a fundamental component of any relationship, whether personal or professional. Our actions play a critical role in building or breaking that trust. Consistently following through on promises, being honest, and showing reliability can help strengthen the trust others have in us. These actions create a foundation of respect and dependability that allows relationships to flourish.

However, actions like dishonesty, inconsistency, or betrayal can damage trust, sometimes irreparably. Once trust is broken, it can be difficult to rebuild, and the consequences of that loss can affect not only the immediate relationship but also future interactions with others. Being mindful of how our actions influence trust encourages us to act with integrity and accountability.

The Role of Empathy and Awareness

Empathy plays a crucial role in understanding how our actions affect others. By putting ourselves in someone else's shoes and considering their perspective, we become more aware of the potential impact of our behavior. This awareness allows us to make choices that are more considerate and aligned with the well-being of others.

Moreover, self-awareness is key to recognizing the ripple effect of our actions. By reflecting on how our behavior influences those around us, we can adjust our actions to create a more positive environment. This not only benefits others but also enhances our own relationships, creating a cycle of compassion and support.

The way we act influences others in ways both visible and unseen. Whether through direct interaction or the ripple effect of our behaviors, our actions have the power to uplift or harm, to build trust or erode it. By becoming more mindful of how our actions affect others, we can cultivate a more positive, empathetic, and compassionate approach to life, enhancing the well-being of everyone we encounter.

Creating a Legacy of Love and Compassion

Creating a legacy of love and compassion is a noble pursuit that transcends individual achievements and material wealth. It involves cultivating relationships, fostering understanding, and leaving a lasting impact on the lives of others. This legacy is not built overnight; rather, it is shaped through consistent actions, intentional choices, and a genuine commitment to making the world a better place for future generations. By embedding love and compassion into our daily lives, we can create a legacy that not only honors our values but also inspires others to follow suit.

Understanding the Importance of Legacy

A legacy is what we leave behind when we are no longer here—an imprint of our beliefs, actions, and values on the world. While many might think of legacy in terms of financial wealth or accomplishments, the most profound legacies are often those rooted in emotional connections and acts of kindness. When we focus on love and compassion, we emphasize the importance of human connection and the impact our behavior has on others. Such a legacy can inspire future generations to prioritize empathy, kindness, and service to others, fostering a ripple effect that can change communities and societies for the better.

Cultivating Compassion in Daily Life

Creating a legacy of love and compassion starts with individual actions. Compassion is more than a feeling; it is an active choice to understand and alleviate the suffering of others. This can be practiced in various ways, such as volunteering for local charities, helping a neighbor in need, or simply offering a listening ear to someone who is struggling.

Moreover, cultivating compassion requires us to become aware of the challenges that others face. This awareness can be developed by engaging in conversations with people from different backgrounds, reading about social issues, and participating in community events. By understanding the diverse experiences of those around us, we can better empathize with their struggles and provide meaningful support.

Leading by Example

One of the most effective ways to create a legacy of love and compassion is to lead by example. Our actions often speak louder than our words, and when we embody the values of kindness and empathy, we inspire others to do the same.

For instance, a parent who demonstrates compassion in their daily interactions is likely to raise children who carry those values into their own lives. Similarly, leaders in the workplace who prioritize employee well-being and foster a supportive environment create a culture of compassion that can endure long after they leave the organization.

Leading by example involves not only demonstrating kindness in our interactions but also encouraging others to embrace these values. This can be done by recognizing and celebrating acts of compassion in our communities, whether big or small. By acknowledging the positive impact of these actions, we reinforce the importance of love and compassion in our collective consciousness.

Building Strong Relationships

Creating a legacy of love and compassion is deeply intertwined with the relationships we build throughout our lives. Strong, meaningful connections with family, friends, and community members provide the foundation for a compassionate legacy. These relationships are built on trust, mutual respect, and a shared commitment to supporting one another.

Investing time in nurturing these relationships is essential. This can include regular communication, spending quality time together, and being present during both good and challenging times. When we prioritize our relationships, we create an environment where love and compassion can thrive.

Additionally, we should strive to extend our compassion beyond our immediate circles. By reaching out to those who may feel isolated or marginalized, we can broaden our impact and foster a more inclusive community. This effort not only enriches the lives of others but also strengthens our own sense of purpose and fulfillment.

The Power of Forgiveness

Forgiveness is a powerful component of creating a legacy of love and compassion. Holding onto grudges or past grievances can hinder our ability to connect with others and cultivate empathy. When we practice forgiveness, we not only release ourselves from the burden of negativity but also create space for healing and reconciliation.

By forgiving others, we model compassion and understanding, demonstrating that everyone makes mistakes and deserves a chance at redemption. This act of letting go can inspire those around us to adopt a similar mindset, fostering a culture of forgiveness within families, friendships, and communities.

Teaching Future Generations

One of the most enduring ways to create a legacy of love and compassion is to teach these values to future generations. This can be done through direct education, storytelling, and shared experiences. By instilling compassion in children from a young age, we equip them with the tools they need to navigate life with empathy and kindness.

Encouraging children to engage in community service, volunteer activities, or acts of kindness not only reinforces these values but also shows them the tangible impact of their actions. Moreover, discussing the importance of love and compassion openly within families helps create a shared understanding of these ideals and their significance.

The Role of Community

Creating a legacy of love and compassion is not solely an individual effort; it is a collective endeavor that requires community involvement. Communities can come together to support one another, whether through organized events, initiatives, or support groups. When people unite to promote kindness and compassion, they amplify their efforts and reach a broader audience.

By participating in community-building activities, we can foster a culture of compassion that encourages individuals to support one another. This can include organizing food drives, community clean-ups, or mental health awareness campaigns. Such initiatives not only address immediate needs but also create an atmosphere of belonging and care, strengthening the bonds among community members.

Creating a legacy of love and compassion is a deeply meaningful pursuit that enriches our lives and the lives of others. By cultivating compassion in our daily actions, leading by example, building strong relationships, practicing forgiveness, and teaching future generations, we can leave an enduring impact on the world. This legacy not only shapes our character but also inspires others to embrace love and compassion, creating a ripple effect that can transform communities and societies for the better.

Ultimately, a legacy of love and compassion is about recognizing our shared humanity and making a conscious effort to support and uplift one another. It is a commitment to living a life rooted in empathy, understanding, and kindness, ensuring that our presence on this earth contributes to a brighter, more compassionate future.

Living a Life That Inspires Future Generations

Living a life that inspires future generations is a profound and rewarding endeavor that requires conscious effort, intention, and a commitment to personal growth and integrity. As we navigate our own lives, the choices we make and the values we uphold have the power to influence those who come after us. By embodying principles such as resilience, kindness, and authenticity, we can create a legacy that not only uplifts others but also encourages them to lead fulfilling lives of their own. This journey involves not only personal development but also active engagement with the community and a dedication to nurturing the next generation.

Embracing Authenticity

One of the foundational elements of living an inspiring life is authenticity. When we embrace who we are, including our strengths and weaknesses, we become relatable and approachable. Authenticity invites others to be themselves, fostering an environment where individuals feel comfortable expressing their true selves. By demonstrating honesty in our actions and choices, we model the importance of self-acceptance and integrity for future generations.

To cultivate authenticity, we must engage in self-reflection and understanding. This involves recognizing our values, beliefs, and passions, which serve as guiding principles in our lives. When we live in alignment with these core values, we inspire others to pursue their passions and embrace their unique identities. Sharing our stories of triumphs and struggles can also resonate with those around us, showing them that vulnerability is a strength and that it's okay to be imperfect.

Fostering Resilience

Resilience is another critical quality that inspires future generations. Life is filled with challenges, setbacks, and adversities, and how we respond to these obstacles sets an example for those who look up to us. By demonstrating resilience, we teach others the importance of perseverance and the value of overcoming difficulties.

To foster resilience, we can share our experiences with failure and how we learned and grew from them. By reframing failures as opportunities for growth, we instill a mindset that embraces challenges rather than shies away from them. Encouraging a culture where resilience is celebrated can empower the next generation to face their own obstacles with confidence and determination.

Nurturing Kindness and Empathy

Kindness and empathy are essential components of a life that inspires others. When we actively practice kindness in our interactions, we create a positive ripple effect that can influence those around us. Simple acts of kindness—whether it's helping a neighbor, volunteering in the community, or offering support to a friend—send a powerful message about the importance of compassion.

Empathy goes hand-in-hand with kindness. By striving to understand others' perspectives and feelings, we promote a culture of connection and support. When future generations witness our empathy in action, they learn the importance of being considerate and compassionate toward others. Encouraging open dialogues about feelings and experiences can cultivate a sense of belonging and acceptance among young people, motivating them to extend kindness to those around them.

Engaging in Lifelong Learning

Living a life that inspires future generations also involves a commitment to lifelong learning. Knowledge is not static; it evolves over time, and so should our understanding of the world. By continually seeking new information, experiences, and skills, we demonstrate that growth is a lifelong journey.

Engaging in lifelong learning allows us to share our insights and wisdom with younger generations. Whether through mentorship, teaching, or simply sharing knowledge in everyday conversations, we can ignite curiosity and encourage a passion for learning in others. By fostering an environment that values education and exploration, we inspire future generations to seek knowledge and remain open to new ideas and experiences.

Leading by Example

Actions often speak louder than words, and leading by example is a powerful way to inspire others. Our behavior, values, and choices set a standard for those who observe us. When we embody the qualities we wish to instill in others—such as integrity, responsibility, and a strong work ethic—we create a model for future generations to follow.

Leading by example also means being accountable for our actions. When we make mistakes, acknowledging them and learning from them teaches resilience and honesty. This transparency creates a safe space for others to embrace their imperfections and grow from their experiences. By demonstrating that it's acceptable to be flawed yet striving for improvement, we encourage future generations to cultivate a growth mindset.

Building Strong Connections

Creating a supportive network of relationships is essential for inspiring future generations. By fostering strong connections with family, friends, mentors, and community members, we create an environment that values collaboration, support, and shared experiences.

These connections provide a safety net for younger generations, allowing them to feel supported and understood. We can facilitate this by encouraging open communication and creating spaces for dialogue, where individuals can share their thoughts, ideas, and challenges. When future generations see the power of collaboration and the importance of building relationships, they are more likely to nurture connections in their own lives.

Leaving a Legacy of Service

Living a life that inspires future generations often involves a commitment to service and giving back to the community. Engaging in volunteer work, supporting charitable initiatives, or simply being present for those in need sends a strong message about the importance of contributing to the greater good.

When we prioritize service, we instill a sense of social responsibility in younger generations. Encouraging them to participate in community service activities helps them develop empathy and a deeper understanding of the challenges faced by others. By demonstrating that our actions can make a positive impact, we inspire future generations to carry on the tradition of service and social responsibility.

Conclusion

Creating a life that inspires future generations is a multifaceted endeavor that requires intention, commitment, and authenticity. By embracing our true selves, fostering resilience, nurturing kindness and empathy, engaging in lifelong learning, leading by example, building strong connections, and prioritizing service, we can leave a lasting legacy that empowers and uplifts those who follow in our footsteps.

As we navigate our own lives, it's essential to recognize the power of our actions and the influence they can have on others. By cultivating a life rooted in love, compassion, and purpose, we not only enrich our own experiences but also create a legacy that inspires future generations to lead lives filled with meaning, connection, and impact. Ultimately, the true measure of our lives lies not in what we achieve for ourselves but in the positive change we inspire in others.

FOURTEEN

Conclusion: Life as a Continuous Learning Process

Life as a Continuous Learning Process

Life is fundamentally a continuous learning process, where each experience serves as a lesson shaping our understanding and growth. From the moment we are born, we embark on a journey filled with opportunities to acquire knowledge, develop skills, and cultivate wisdom. This journey is not confined to formal education; rather, it encompasses every interaction, challenge, and moment of reflection we encounter.

As we navigate through different stages of life, we learn valuable lessons about ourselves and the world around us. Mistakes become stepping stones to growth, teaching us resilience and adaptability. Each triumph, no matter how small, reinforces our capabilities and encourages us to pursue new challenges.

Moreover, learning is not a solitary endeavor. Engaging with others—friends, family, mentors, or even strangers—provides diverse perspectives that enrich our understanding. This exchange of ideas fosters empathy and broadens our worldview, reminding us that learning is a shared experience.

In embracing life as a continuous learning process, we cultivate a growth mindset that allows us to remain open to new experiences and insights. This mindset empowers us to embrace change, adapt to new circumstances, and ultimately lead more fulfilling lives. By valuing learning, we transform our journey into an ongoing adventure of discovery and growth.

Embracing the Never-Ending Journey of Growth

Growth is a fundamental aspect of the human experience, characterized by the continuous evolution of our thoughts, beliefs, and behaviors. Embracing this never-ending journey of growth means recognizing that life is an ongoing process of learning and development. It invites us to be open to change, adapt to new circumstances, and cultivate a mindset that welcomes challenges as opportunities for improvement.

At the heart of this journey is the understanding that growth is not a destination but a process. Each stage of life presents unique experiences that shape our perspectives and contribute to our personal evolution. Whether it's navigating the complexities of relationships, advancing in our careers, or simply reflecting on our values, every moment provides a chance to learn and grow. By embracing this notion, we shift our focus from achieving specific milestones to appreciating the journey itself.

One of the essential components of embracing growth is cultivating a growth mindset, a concept popularized by psychologist Carol Dweck. A growth mindset encourages us to view challenges as opportunities rather than obstacles. When faced with difficulties, those with a growth mindset are more likely to persevere, seek solutions, and learn from their experiences. This perspective fosters resilience, enabling us to bounce back from setbacks and emerge stronger.

Additionally, embracing the journey of growth involves self-reflection. Taking time to assess our experiences, thoughts, and emotions allows us to gain valuable insights into our behaviors and motivations. Self-reflection fosters self-awareness, which is crucial for personal development. It helps us identify areas for improvement and recognize patterns that may hinder our progress. By engaging in regular self-reflection, we become more attuned to our growth, making it easier to embrace the changes that come our way.

Another vital aspect of growth is the willingness to step outside our comfort zones. Growth often occurs when we challenge ourselves to take risks and try new things. Whether it's pursuing a new hobby, taking on a challenging project at work, or engaging in difficult conversations, stepping outside our comfort zones fosters resilience and builds confidence. Each experience, no matter the outcome, contributes to our growth and expands our horizons.

Furthermore, embracing the journey of growth means surrounding ourselves with supportive and inspiring individuals. Relationships play a significant role in our development, providing encouragement, accountability, and diverse perspectives. Engaging with others who share a growth mindset can be particularly motivating. These relationships can challenge us to reach our potential and offer guidance and support when navigating obstacles.

It's also essential to recognize that growth is not linear; it often involves ups and downs. There will be times of rapid progress, followed by periods of stagnation or regression. Acknowledging this natural ebb and flow can help us remain patient and compassionate toward ourselves. It's crucial to celebrate our successes, no matter how small, and recognize that setbacks are not failures but rather integral parts of the growth process.

In addition to personal growth, embracing the journey extends to our professional lives. The world is constantly changing, driven by technological advancements and shifting societal norms. To thrive in this dynamic environment, we must remain adaptable and willing to learn. Continuous professional development—whether through formal education, training, or self-directed learning—ensures that we are equipped to meet new challenges and seize opportunities.

Lastly, embracing the never-ending journey of growth means fostering a sense of curiosity and wonder. Cultivating a love for learning enriches our lives and encourages us to explore new ideas, cultures, and experiences. This curiosity fuels our desire to grow, prompting us to seek knowledge and expand our understanding of the world.

In conclusion, embracing the never-ending journey of growth is about more than personal development; it's about living a life rich with meaning and purpose. By adopting a growth mindset, engaging in self-reflection, stepping outside our comfort zones, fostering supportive relationships, and remaining curious, we can navigate life's challenges with resilience and grace. Ultimately, the journey of growth enriches our lives and allows us to contribute positively to the world around us, inspiring others to embark on their own paths of growth.

Learning from Every Experience

Life is a tapestry woven from countless experiences, each offering unique lessons and insights. Embracing the philosophy of learning from every experience transforms the way we perceive challenges, successes, and failures. This approach allows us to extract valuable knowledge from our daily interactions, encounters, and even the mundane aspects of life, fostering personal growth and resilience.

At its core, the idea of learning from every experience encourages us to adopt a reflective mindset. Reflection involves looking back on our experiences with a critical eye, analyzing our thoughts, feelings, and reactions. This process of introspection can illuminate patterns in our behavior, reveal underlying beliefs, and provide clarity on how we can improve. By taking the time to reflect, we create an opportunity to distill meaningful lessons from both positive and negative experiences.

One of the most significant aspects of this learning journey is understanding that failures and setbacks are not merely obstacles but rather essential components of growth. When we face difficulties, it's easy to fall into the trap of self-doubt or frustration. However, viewing these moments as opportunities to learn can shift our perspective dramatically. For instance, a job rejection might initially feel disheartening, but it can also prompt us to evaluate our skills, refine our approach, and explore new opportunities that we might not have considered otherwise.

Moreover, learning from every experience also extends to our relationships with others. Interactions with family, friends, colleagues, and even strangers can provide profound insights into human behavior, communication, and empathy. Each conversation, conflict, or shared moment can teach us about ourselves and others, helping us develop emotional intelligence and deeper connections. For example, navigating a disagreement with a friend can reveal not only differing perspectives but also the importance of active listening and compromise. These relational lessons contribute to our overall growth as individuals.

Furthermore, embracing the idea of learning from every experience encourages us to cultivate a sense of curiosity about the world around us. When we approach life with an open mind, we are more likely to seek out new experiences and perspectives. This curiosity can lead us to explore diverse cultures, engage with new ideas, and step outside our comfort zones. Each new experience enriches our understanding of the world and broadens our horizons. For instance, traveling to a new country exposes us to different customs, values, and ways of life, challenging our preconceived notions and encouraging us to embrace diversity.

In addition to curiosity, maintaining a growth mindset is essential for learning from experiences. This concept, popularized by psychologist Carol Dweck, emphasizes the belief that abilities and intelligence can be developed through effort and perseverance. When we adopt a growth mindset, we view challenges as opportunities for learning rather than insurmountable barriers. This mindset allows us to remain resilient in the face of setbacks and encourages us to persist in our endeavors. For example, a student who struggles with a particular subject may initially feel discouraged, but by embracing a growth mindset, they can seek help, practice more, and ultimately improve their understanding.

Another vital aspect of learning from every experience is the importance of gratitude. Recognizing the lessons embedded in our experiences, both good and bad, fosters a sense of appreciation for the journey. Gratitude shifts our focus from what went wrong to what we can learn and how we can grow. This perspective not only enhances our emotional well-being but also encourages a positive outlook on life. By practicing gratitude, we cultivate resilience and develop a greater capacity to navigate future challenges.

Finally, the practice of sharing our experiences with others can further enhance our learning journey. When we communicate our lessons and insights, we not only reinforce our understanding but also provide value to those around us. Sharing stories of triumph and adversity can inspire others and foster a sense of community. For example, a mentor who shares their experiences with their mentees can provide valuable guidance and encouragement, creating a supportive environment for growth.

In conclusion, learning from every experience is a powerful philosophy that enriches our lives and contributes to our personal development. By adopting a reflective mindset, embracing failures, nurturing curiosity, maintaining a growth mindset, practicing gratitude, and sharing our insights with others, we can transform our experiences into valuable lessons. This approach not only enhances our resilience and emotional intelligence but also prepares us to navigate the complexities of life with confidence and grace. Ultimately, each experience, whether positive or negative, is an opportunity for growth, and by embracing this journey, we can lead more fulfilling and meaningful lives.

The Wisdom of Letting Go and Moving Forward

In the intricate tapestry of life, one of the most profound lessons we can learn is the art of letting go. This wisdom involves releasing attachments, emotions, and beliefs that no longer serve us, enabling us to move forward with clarity and purpose. Letting go is not merely an act of surrender; it is a powerful choice that allows us to create space for new experiences, personal growth, and emotional well-being.

The Nature of Attachment

To understand the wisdom of letting go, it's essential to recognize the nature of attachment. Human beings naturally form attachments to people, places, experiences, and even outcomes. These attachments can provide comfort and security, creating a sense of belonging and identity. However, when we cling too tightly to these attachments, we risk becoming stagnant, weighed down by the past, and unable to embrace change. This is particularly true when attachments become burdensome, causing us pain, stress, or dissatisfaction.

For instance, consider a friendship that has become toxic. Initially, this relationship may have brought joy and support, but over time, it may shift to one marked by negativity or conflict. Holding on to such a relationship out of fear of loneliness or the unknown can prevent us from pursuing healthier connections. In these moments, letting go becomes an act of self-care, freeing us from what no longer nourishes our spirit.

The Process of Letting Go

Letting go is often a complex and emotional process. It requires introspection, self-awareness, and courage. The first step in this journey is acknowledging the need to release something from our lives. This acknowledgment may come from recognizing feelings of dissatisfaction, discomfort, or unhappiness that arise from holding onto past experiences, relationships, or beliefs.

Once we identify what needs to be let go, the next step is to explore the emotions tied to those attachments. Fear, grief, guilt, and uncertainty are common feelings that arise when we contemplate letting go. It's important to validate these emotions and allow ourselves to feel them fully. Denying or suppressing our feelings can lead to deeper emotional distress. Instead, embracing these feelings as part of the process can help us navigate the complexities of letting go.

For example, when grieving the loss of a loved one, allowing ourselves to feel sadness, anger, or confusion is a crucial aspect of healing. This emotional acknowledgment can eventually pave the way for acceptance and moving forward, creating space for new experiences and relationships to flourish.

The Freedom in Letting Go

One of the most significant aspects of letting go is the freedom it brings. By releasing attachments, we create room for new opportunities, perspectives, and experiences. This newfound freedom can lead to personal growth and self-discovery, enabling us to pursue passions and interests that may have been overshadowed by our previous attachments.

Moreover, letting go can significantly enhance our emotional well-being. Clinging to past hurt, regret, or resentment can drain our energy and hinder our ability to fully engage in the present. When we release these burdens, we free ourselves from the chains of our past, allowing us to embrace the beauty and possibilities of the present moment.

Moving Forward with Intent

Letting go is not just about releasing what no longer serves us; it is also about moving forward with intention. Once we have released our attachments, it's essential to redirect our focus toward what we want to cultivate in our lives. This proactive approach involves setting new goals, pursuing passions, and seeking out meaningful connections.

Moving forward with intent requires self-reflection and clarity. Taking the time to evaluate our values, desires, and aspirations can help us determine what aligns with our true selves. By identifying what we want to create or achieve, we can navigate our path with purpose and determination.

For instance, someone who has let go of a long-standing career that no longer fulfills them might take the opportunity to explore new professional avenues that resonate with their passions. This shift not only brings a sense of excitement but also aligns with their desire for a more meaningful and rewarding life.

Cultivating Resilience

The wisdom of letting go and moving forward also involves cultivating resilience. Life is full of uncertainties, and setbacks are inevitable. By embracing the practice of letting go, we become more adaptable and open to change, allowing us to face challenges with a sense of hope and determination.

Resilience is strengthened through our experiences of letting go. Each time we release something that no longer serves us, we learn to trust ourselves and our ability to navigate the unknown. This self-trust empowers us to take risks, explore new opportunities, and face challenges with confidence.

The Journey of Self-Discovery

Ultimately, the wisdom of letting go and moving forward is a journey of self-discovery. As we release attachments, we gain a deeper understanding of ourselves and our values. This process fosters personal growth, leading us to explore new dimensions of our identity and purpose.

Through letting go, we uncover hidden strengths, passions, and desires that may have been buried beneath the weight of our attachments. This self-discovery not only enhances our sense of self but also empowers us to create a life that reflects our true essence.

In conclusion, the wisdom of letting go and moving forward is a transformative journey that invites us to release what no longer serves us and embrace new possibilities. By recognizing the nature of attachment, engaging in the process of letting go, and moving forward with intention, we open ourselves to a life rich with opportunities for growth, resilience, and self-discovery. Ultimately, letting go is not a sign of weakness; it is an act of courage that paves the way for a brighter, more fulfilling future.

Appendix: Practical Exercises For Personal Growth

Personal growth is a lifelong journey that can be significantly enhanced through practical exercises. These exercises can help individuals cultivate self-awareness, resilience, and a sense of purpose. Here are a few effective methods to foster personal development:

1. **Journaling**: Dedicate time each day to write about your thoughts, feelings, and experiences. Reflecting on your day can help identify patterns in your behavior and emotions, facilitating self-discovery and clarity.
2. **Goal Setting**: Create SMART (Specific, Measurable, Achievable, Relevant, Time-bound) goals. Breaking down larger ambitions into smaller, actionable steps can make achieving them more manageable and motivating.
3. **Mindfulness Meditation**: Practice mindfulness to enhance your awareness of the present moment. Spend a few minutes each day focusing on your breath or observing your thoughts without judgment. This can reduce stress and increase emotional resilience.
4. **Seeking Feedback**: Regularly ask for constructive feedback from friends, family, or colleagues. This can provide valuable insights into your strengths and areas for improvement, fostering personal and professional growth.
5. **Reading and Learning**: Engage with books, podcasts, or online courses related to personal development. Learning new concepts and strategies can inspire you and broaden your perspective, enriching your growth journey.

By integrating these exercises into your daily routine, you can cultivate a deeper understanding of yourself and actively pursue personal growth.

Journaling Prompts for Self-Reflection

Journaling is a powerful tool for self-reflection and personal growth. It allows you to explore your thoughts, emotions, and experiences in a structured way. Here are some journaling prompts designed to guide your self-reflection and deepen your understanding of yourself:

1. Daily Reflection

- What are three things I am grateful for today?
- What did I learn about myself today?
- What emotions did I experience today, and what triggered them?

2. Personal Values

- What values are most important to me, and how do they influence my decisions?
- How do I align my daily actions with my core values?
- What changes can I make to live more in alignment with my values?

3. Goals and Aspirations

- What are my short-term and long-term goals?
- What steps can I take this week to move closer to achieving one of my goals?
- What obstacles have I encountered in pursuing my goals, and how can I overcome them?

4. Relationships

- Who are the most important people in my life, and why?
- How do my relationships contribute to my happiness and growth?
- What can I do to strengthen my connections with others?

5. Strengths and Weaknesses

- What are my greatest strengths, and how do I utilize them in my life?
- What weaknesses would I like to work on, and how can I address them?
- How can I leverage my strengths to overcome my weaknesses?

6. Challenges and Resilience

- What challenges have I faced recently, and what have I learned from them?
- How do I typically respond to adversity, and how can I improve my resilience?
- What strategies have helped me cope with difficult situations in the past?

7. Dreams and Aspirations

- What are my dreams for the future, and what steps can I take to pursue them?
- What fears or doubts hold me back from chasing my dreams?
- What would I attempt if I knew I could not fail?

8. Self-Compassion

- How do I practice self-compassion in my daily life?
- What negative self-talk do I need to challenge, and how can I reframe those thoughts?
- What is one kind thing I can say to myself today?

9. Lessons Learned

- What is the most valuable lesson I have learned in the past year?
- How have my experiences shaped who I am today?
- What advice would I give to my younger self?

10. Future Vision

- Where do I see myself in five years?
- What legacy do I want to leave behind?
- What steps can I take today to work toward my vision for the future?

How to Use These Prompts

1. **Choose a Prompt**: Select one prompt that resonates with you. You can choose a prompt daily, weekly, or whenever you feel the need for self-reflection.
2. **Set Aside Time**: Find a quiet space where you can write without distractions. Allocate a specific amount of time for journaling, whether it's 10 minutes or an hour.
3. **Write Freely**: Don't worry about grammar or structure; let your thoughts flow naturally. Allow yourself to be honest and open in your writing.
4. **Reflect on Your Writing**: After you've completed a prompt, take a moment to read over what you've written. Consider any patterns or

insights that emerge.

5. **Review Regularly**: Set aside time to review your previous entries. This can help you track your progress, recognize patterns, and celebrate your growth.

By using these journaling prompts for self-reflection, you can cultivate a deeper understanding of yourself, foster personal growth, and enhance your emotional well-being.

Mindfulness Practices for Daily Life

Incorporating mindfulness into your daily routine can significantly enhance your overall well-being, reduce stress, and improve your focus. Here's an exercise designed to help you practice mindfulness in various aspects of your day:

Exercise: Mindfulness Practices for Daily Life

1. Mindful Breathing (5-10 minutes)

- **Find a Comfortable Space**: Sit or lie down in a comfortable position where you won't be disturbed.
- **Focus on Your Breath**: Close your eyes and take a deep breath in through your nose, allowing your abdomen to expand. Hold it for a moment, then exhale slowly through your mouth.
- **Count Your Breaths**: Inhale for a count of four, hold for four, and exhale for six. Repeat this for several cycles. If your mind starts to wander, gently bring your focus back to your breath.
- **Reflect**: After a few minutes, take a moment to notice how you feel. Are there any changes in your body or mind?

2. Mindful Eating (15-20 minutes)

- **Choose a Meal or Snack**: Pick a meal or snack to eat mindfully.
- **Engage Your Senses**: Before you eat, take a moment to observe the colors, textures, and smells of the food.
- **Eat Slowly**: Take a small bite and chew slowly, savoring the flavors. Pay attention to the sensations in your mouth and how the food feels as you chew and swallow.
- **Reflect**: After finishing your meal, take a moment to appreciate the nourishment it provides. How did this experience differ from your usual eating habits?

3. Mindful Walking (10-15 minutes)

- **Find a Suitable Place**: Choose a quiet area where you can walk without distractions, such as a park or a quiet street.
- **Focus on Your Steps**: As you walk, pay attention to the sensation of your feet touching the ground. Notice the rhythm of your steps and the movement of your body.
- **Observe Your Surroundings**: Take in the sights, sounds, and smells around you. Notice the colors of the leaves, the sound of birds, or the feeling of the breeze on your skin.
- **Reflect**: After your walk, pause for a moment to acknowledge how you feel. Did you notice anything new in your environment?

4. Mindful Listening (5-10 minutes)

- **Choose a Sound**: Find a quiet space where you can listen without distractions. This could be a piece of music, nature sounds, or even the ambient noise of your surroundings.
- **Close Your Eyes**: Close your eyes and focus entirely on the sound. Notice its pitch, volume, and any changes in rhythm.
- **Stay Present**: If your mind wanders, gently bring your attention back to the sound. Observe your reactions and feelings as you listen.
- **Reflect**: After a few minutes, think about how this experience of listening differed from your usual way of hearing sounds in your environment.

5. Mindful Journaling (10-15 minutes)

- **Set a Timer**: Choose a prompt related to your day or your feelings and set a timer for 10-15 minutes.
- **Write Freely**: Write down your thoughts, emotions, or observations without worrying about grammar or structure. Allow yourself to express whatever comes to mind.
- **Practice Awareness**: As you write, notice any physical sensations or emotions that arise. Acknowledge them without judgment.
- **Reflect**: After you finish writing, read over what you've written and consider any insights you gained about yourself.

Tips for Integrating Mindfulness into Daily Life

1. **Start Small**: Begin by incorporating short mindfulness exercises into your daily routine and gradually increase the duration as you become more comfortable.
2. **Be Consistent**: Try to practice mindfulness at the same time each day, whether in the morning, during lunch, or before bed.
3. **Use Reminders**: Set reminders on your phone or place sticky notes in your living space to prompt you to take mindfulness breaks throughout the day.
4. **Stay Patient**: Mindfulness is a skill that develops over time. Be patient with yourself and acknowledge that it's normal for your mind to wander.
5. **Make It Fun**: Choose activities that you enjoy, such as cooking, gardening, or exercising, and practice mindfulness during those moments.

By integrating these mindfulness practices into your daily life, you can cultivate a greater sense of presence, enhance your emotional well-being, and foster a deeper connection to yourself and the world around you

Exercise: Mindfulness Practices for Daily Life

Incorporating mindfulness into your daily routine can enhance your well-being, reduce stress, and improve your focus. Here's a structured exercise designed to help you practice mindfulness in various aspects of your day:

Overview of the Exercise

Goal: To cultivate mindfulness through everyday activities.

Duration: 30-60 minutes (can be spread throughout the day).

Materials Needed:

- A journal or notepad
- Comfortable clothing (for movement or relaxation)
- A quiet space

Step 1: Mindful Morning Routine (10-15 minutes)

Practice:

1. **Awaken with Intention**: As soon as you wake up, take a moment to notice your breath. Before getting out of bed, spend a few minutes in silence, focusing on your breathing.
2. **Mindful Hygiene**: As you brush your teeth, wash your face, or shower,

pay attention to the sensations. Notice the temperature of the water, the feeling of the toothbrush on your teeth, and the scents of your soap or shampoo.

3. **Set an Intention for the Day**: Take a moment to reflect on what you want to focus on today. Write down one intention or goal in your journal.

Step 2: Mindful Eating (15-20 minutes)
Practice:

1. **Choose a Meal or Snack**: Select a meal or snack to eat mindfully, preferably one that you can enjoy without distractions.
2. **Engage Your Senses**: Before eating, observe the colors, textures, and smells of the food. Acknowledge the effort that went into preparing it.
3. **Eat Slowly**: Take a small bite and chew slowly, savoring the flavors. Put down your utensils between bites and focus on the act of eating.
4. **Reflect**: After finishing, write down in your journal how this experience felt compared to your usual eating habits.

Step 3: Mindful Movement (10-15 minutes)
Practice:

1. **Choose a Movement**: This could be walking, stretching, yoga, or any form of exercise.
2. **Focus on Your Body**: As you move, pay attention to how your body feels. Notice the muscles you engage and how your breath changes with each movement.
3. **Be Present**: If your mind wanders, gently bring your focus back to your body and your movements.
4. **Reflect**: After your movement session, jot down any feelings or thoughts in your journal. Did this practice shift your mood or energy?

Step 4: Mindful Listening (5-10 minutes)
Practice:

1. **Find a Quiet Space**: Choose a place where you can listen without distractions.
2. **Close Your Eyes**: Focus on the sounds around you—birds chirping, wind rustling, or background music.

3. **Stay Present**: If your mind drifts, gently redirect your attention back to the sounds. Notice how they make you feel.
4. **Reflect**: Write about the experience in your journal. How did it feel to listen without judgment or distraction?

Step 5: Evening Reflection (10-15 minutes)
Practice:

1. **Settle into a Comfortable Space**: At the end of the day, find a quiet spot where you can reflect.
2. **Reflect on Your Day**: Think about moments of mindfulness you experienced. What went well? What challenges did you face?
3. **Write in Your Journal**: Note any insights you gained, what you're grateful for, and how you felt throughout the day.
4. **Plan for Tomorrow**: Consider how you might incorporate more mindfulness into your routine tomorrow.

Tips for Incorporating Mindfulness into Daily Life

- **Be Consistent**: Try to practice mindfulness at the same time each day to create a habit.
- **Use Reminders**: Set reminders on your phone or place sticky notes around your home to prompt mindfulness breaks.
- **Stay Patient**: Understand that mindfulness is a practice; it's normal for your mind to wander. Gently bring your focus back when it does.
- **Make It Enjoyable**: Choose activities you enjoy for your mindfulness practice, making it a positive experience.

By integrating these mindfulness practices into your daily life, you can cultivate greater awareness, reduce stress, and enhance your emotional well-being.

Exercise: Building Better Relationships through Active Listening

Active listening is a powerful skill that enhances communication, strengthens relationships, and fosters understanding. This exercise is designed to help you practice active listening in your interactions with others, whether in personal or professional contexts.

Overview of the Exercise

Goal: To develop active listening skills that improve relationships and communication.

Duration: 30-60 minutes (can be divided into multiple interactions).

Materials Needed:

- A journal or notepad for reflection
- A comfortable space for conversation

Step-by-Step Active Listening Exercise

Step 1: Prepare for Active Listening (5 minutes)

1. **Create a Comfortable Environment**: Find a quiet space where you can have an uninterrupted conversation. Ensure both you and the other person feel comfortable.
2. **Set an Intention**: Before the conversation, take a moment to reflect on your intention. Remind yourself that your goal is to listen fully and understand the other person's perspective.

Step 2: Engage in a Conversation (15-20 minutes)

1. **Choose a Conversation Partner**: Select a friend, family member, or colleague who is open to engaging in a meaningful conversation. You can also practice with someone you're comfortable with, like a family member or a close friend.
2. **Start the Conversation**: Invite your partner to share their thoughts or feelings on a topic of their choice. It could be something they're passionate about, a recent experience, or any subject they'd like to discuss.
3. **Listen Actively**: As they speak, practice the following active listening techniques:

    - **Maintain Eye Contact**: Show that you're engaged and interested in what they're saying.
    - **Use Non-Verbal Cues**: Nod and use facial expressions to demonstrate understanding and empathy.
    - **Avoid Interrupting**: Allow them to express their thoughts fully without interrupting or jumping in with your own opinions.
    - **Paraphrase and Reflect**: After they finish speaking, paraphrase what

they said to confirm your understanding. For example, "So, what I hear you saying is..."

- **Ask Open-Ended Questions**: Encourage them to elaborate by asking questions like, "How did that make you feel?" or "What do you think about...?"

Step 3: Switch Roles (15-20 minutes)

1. **Reverse Roles**: After the first conversation, switch roles with your partner. Now, it's your turn to share your thoughts while your partner practices active listening.
2. **Share Your Perspective**: Discuss a topic that's important to you, following the same guidelines for open communication.
3. **Practice Active Listening Techniques**: As your partner listens, notice how it feels to be heard and understood. This can deepen your appreciation for the active listening process.

Step 4: Reflect on the Experience (10-15 minutes)

1. **Journaling**: After both conversations, take some time to reflect on your experience in your journal. Consider the following prompts:

   - How did it feel to practice active listening?
   - Did you notice any changes in how you communicated or understood the other person?
   - How did your partner respond to your active listening?
   - What challenges did you face while trying to listen actively?
   - What did you learn about the importance of listening in building relationships?

2. **Discuss Your Insights**: If possible, have a brief discussion with your partner about the experience. Share what you learned from each other and how you can both improve your listening skills in the future.

Tips for Improving Active Listening Skills

- **Stay Present**: Focus fully on the speaker, avoiding distractions like phones or other devices.

- **Practice Empathy**: Try to put yourself in the other person's shoes to understand their feelings and perspectives better.
- **Be Patient**: Allow pauses in the conversation. Sometimes, the most meaningful insights come after a moment of silence.
- **Avoid Judgment**: Listen without jumping to conclusions or forming judgments. Accept their feelings and thoughts as valid, even if you disagree.
- **Follow Up**: After the conversation, consider checking in with your partner later to show that you care about what they shared.

By regularly practicing active listening, you can build stronger relationships, enhance your communication skills, and create a deeper sense of connection with others

www.ingramcontent.com/pod-product-compliance
Lightning Source LLC
LaVergne TN
LVHW091320150826
845673LV00006B/1705

* 9 7 9 8 8 9 5 8 8 4 3 3 1 *